# KHUSHWANT SINGH On *Religion*

Born in Punjab's Hadali village (now in Pakistan) in 1915, Khushwant Singh has acquired an iconic stature: he is, arguably, India's best-known and most widely read author, columnist and journalist. He was founder-editor of *Yojana*, and editor of *The Illustrated Weekly of India*, *National Herald* and the *Hindustan Times*. His first book, *The Mark of Vishnu and Other Stories*, was published in 1950. Among his best-known works today include the novels *Train to Pakistan*, *I Shall Not Hear the Nightingale* and *Delhi*; his autobiography, *Truth, Love and a Little Malice*; and the two-volume *A History of the Sikhs*.

Khushwant Singh was member of the Rajya Sabha from 1980 to 1986. He was awarded the Padma Bhushan in 1974; he returned the award in 1984 to protest the siege of the Golden Temple by the Indian Army. In 2007, he was awarded India's second highest civilian honour, the Padma Vibhushan.

Khushwant Singh died in 2014.

# KHUSHWANT SINGH
{with Humra Quraishi}

## On Religion

~ SELECTED WRITINGS ~

RUPA

Published by
Rupa Publications India Pvt. Ltd 2014
7/16, Ansari Road, Daryaganj
New Delhi 110002

*Sales centres:*
Allahabad Bengaluru Chennai
Hyderabad Jaipur Kathmandu
Kolkata Mumbai

Copyright © Mala Dayal and Naina Dayal 2014
Edition copyright © Rupa Publications India 2014

The views and opinions expressed in this book are the author's
own and the facts are as reported by him, which have been
verified to the extent possible, and the publishers are
not in any way liable for the same.

All rights reserved.
No part of this publication may be reproduced, transmitted, or
stored in a retrieval system, in any form or by any means,
electronic, mechanical, photocopying, recording or otherwise,
without the prior permission of the publisher.

ISBN: 978-81-291-3502-5

10 9 8 7 6 5 4 3 2 1

First impression 2014

The moral right of the author has been asserted.

Typeset in IowanOldST BT by SÜRYA, New Delhi

Printed at Replika Press Pvt. Ltd, India

This book is sold subject to the condition that it shall not,
by way of trade or otherwise, be lent, resold, hired out,
or otherwise circulated, without the publisher's prior consent,
in any form of binding or cover other than that in
which it is published.

# CONTENTS

| | |
|---|---:|
| Religion: A Personal View | 1 |
| A Good Life Is the Only True Religion | 49 |
| The Power of Prayer and Miracles | 81 |
| Being an Agnostic | 98 |
| A Just God? | 102 |
| The Question of Morality | 105 |
| God on Sale | 112 |
| The Question of Reason | 117 |
| With the Devout | 120 |
| A Competition | 124 |

## CONTENTS

| | |
|---|---|
| Sikhism | 130 |
| The Dalai Lama | 151 |
| A Monk with Good Taste | 160 |
| Guru Nanak | 165 |
| Kabir | 187 |
| Shraddha Mata | 191 |
| Mother Valikamma | 197 |
| After Life | 202 |
| *Acknowledgements* | 206 |

# RELIGION: A PERSONAL VIEW

Have you seen God? No, I have not. Nor do I believe that anyone, at any time, past or present, has seen Him. As for me, even if I come face to face with Him, I would not recognize him. Were He to give me His visiting card and say, 'I am "God",' I would say in utter disbelief, 'Tell me another.'

However, there have been, and are today, people who claim to have seen Him and can give graphic descriptions of Him. I am not talking of people who give airy-fairy answers like, 'God is everywhere; you only have to have eyes to see him,' or, as is more common now, 'God is within you.' No X-ray of the human body shows the presence of anything resembling God. 'God is truth; God is love,' say many others, as did Bapu Gandhi. I do not know what truth and love look like—one is a principle of social behaviour, the other an emotion.

In our country most people believe in gods taking human form. There is, of course, the trinity of Brahma, Vishnu and Mahesh (Creator, Preserver and Destroyer), but that is more of a concept of divinity than people who are visible. To many Hindus, Rama was, and is, God. To others it is Krishna. Many believe Satya Sai Baba was God incarnate; others believe Osho was bhagwan. All were and are mortals, some have gone, others are on their way out. Yet everyone insists that God is immortal. I am baffled.

For whatever they're worth, some people have given vivid descriptions of what God looks like. He is invariably portrayed as a patriarch with a flowing snow-white beard, in His sixties or seventies. Did He age over the years or was He always an old man? Perhaps by depicting Him as old the artist meant to convey wisdom and experience.

Some of the Old Testament prophets claimed to have seen God. Ezekiel describes Him thus: 'Above the firmament that was over their heads was the likeness of a throne, as the appearance of a sapphire stone: and upon the likeness of the throne was the likeness as the appearance of a man above upon it. And I saw as the colour of amber, as the appearance of fire round about within it...and it had brightness round about. As the appearance of the bow that is in the cloud in the day of rain, so was the appearance of the brightness round about. This was the appearance of the likeness of the glory of the Lord.'

## RELIGION: A PERSONAL VIEW

Daniel added his own description: 'The Ancient of days did sit, whose garment was white as snow, and the hair of his head like the pure wool: his throne was like the fiery flame, and his wheels as burning fire.' The poet-painter, William Blake, painted God as the venerable father of humanity.

Our sacred scriptures do not venture to depict God. Even Krishna's self-portrait in the Gita, extolling His omniscience and omnipotence, does not describe His physical features. The one thing that all descriptions of divinity have in common is light at its most dazzling.

There is also a charming description of God in Bhai Bula's *Janamsakhi* (life story) of Guru Nanak, which scholars have spurned as spurious and written much after the guru. It describes God as a long-bearded old man draped in white clothes, sitting on an ornate charpoy, and surrounded by fat buffaloes bursting with milk—a peasant's concept of a rich Punjabi zamindar.

Right from the time life began on earth people have been asking themselves who or what made us, what was His, Her or Its purpose, where do we go, when do we die. Nobody has yet been able to give satisfactory answers to these questions. It seems no one will ever be able to do so. All we have are assertions about a God who one fine day decided to create life, gave different creatures different names, different spans of life and then made them disappear forever. At first they conjectured that the elements that created life—the sun, rain, earth, air, etc.—were their creator's and therefore worthy of worship. They raised temples in their honour. Some time later, people thought there must be hundreds of thousands of creators who looked after different aspects of life; others argued there should be one creator. They called it God. Still later came philosophers and prophets. Philosophers speculated on the origin and purpose of life; Prophets asserted they knew the ultimate truth. In the Middle East we had Zoroaster, Abraham and Moses, Jesus Christ and Mohammed. Then, followers banded themselves into separate groups and sought to impose their views on others. In India we had Mahavir and Gautam the Buddha. Neither really accepted the existence of a God but laid down norms of societal behaviour and acquired large followings. Their predominance was challenged by Adi Shankara who was able to re-establish Hindu predominance.

Different religions, though they preached love and brotherhood of mankind, fought wars against each other. In India the inroads made by non-Indian religions like Christianity and Islam posed serious challenges to the caste-ossified Hindu society. These challenges were met in battlefields as well as in attempts to come to an understanding between each other. From the Hindu side they were the Bhaktas (notably Kabir and Nanak); from the Muslim, Sufis, notably Farid, Muinuddin and Nizamuddin of the Chishtia order. The process of coming to an understanding between contending faiths has continued.

Perhaps the most-quoted lines to prove that Islam accepts the validity of other faiths is: 'To you your faith, to me mine.' Nevertheless it cannot be denied that the two religions most engaged in converting other people to their beliefs are Islam and Christianity.

They assume they have more viable answers to vital questions; the existence of the creator, the purpose of life, the codes of conduct to be observed towards our fellow creatures, life after death—if there is any—than other religions. Whether or not this is so remains to be established.

At some time or the other in their lives, all humans ask themselves these questions. Most often it happens when they lie on their backs on moonless nights gazing at the countless stars that stretch across the black sky. 'Where have they come from?' they ask. 'Where have I come from?'

Most often it is people who live in deserts, undisturbed by electric lights and city noises, and sleep in the open under the deafening silence of the stars, whose minds are triggered off to ponder over these problems. That is why so many of the prophets were people of deserts or waste lands.

All Semitic religions believe that God is one: so do Sikhs and Arya Samajis. Most Hindus believe in the multiplicity of gods and goddesses but give the trinity of Brahma, Vishnu and Shiva supreme status; Jains and Buddhists discard belief in God.

Most religions that subscribe to God make Him the Creator, Preserver and Destroyer of life. They also believe in life after death—either in the form of the day of judgement or as rebirth. However, though Islam preaches belief in one God and in the day of judgement, Muslim poets do not hesitate to express their disbelief in either the genesis of life or in the day of judgement.

To quote Omar Khayyam:

> Into this world and why not knowing
> And like water willy-nilly flowing.

He admitted that he did not understand the mystery of life and death:

> There was a door to which I found no key,
> There was a veil beyond which I could not see;
> Talk awhile of thee and me there was
> Then no more of thee or me.

Ghalib, Zauq and other Urdu poets expressed similar beliefs. Azim Jahanabadi put it succinctly: Na ibtada ki khabar hai, na intihaa maaloom—we know not the beginning, we know not the end.

## RELIGION: A PERSONAL VIEW

Although we have to concede that if the earth exists, somebody or some force must have created it and maintains it for whatever it is worth. As Voltaire said, If there is a watch, there must be a watchmaker. The analogy is misleading because while we can trace the watchmaker, the world-maker remains as elusive as ever. To wit:

> Tu dil mein to aata hai
> Samajh mein nahin aata;
> Bas jaan gayaa yehi hai pehechaan teri.
>
> (The heart believes You are there
> The brain does not comprehend You;
> That perhaps is the only way of knowing You.)

Why not be honest and admit we don't know whether God exists or not?

Epicurus (circa 300 BC) was a Greek philosopher who denied the existence of God and emphasized that since we do not know why we were born, for what purpose, and know nothing about what would happen to us after we die, we should enjoy life as best as we can. Epicureanism was later summed up as a motto: eat, drink and be merry, for tomorrow we may die. It is also known as hedonism, the philosophy of good living.

We have been very unfair to Epicurus by equating his beliefs with an amoral way of living. In rejecting the existence of God, he made a series of assertions, for which

I cannot find the answers. All God-believers (theists) affirm that the world was created by God (exactly when, we do not know), that He is omnipotent (sarvshaktimaan) as well as merciful (raheem), just (aadil) and has compassion (karuna). Epicurus argues as follows:

> If God is willing to prevent evil, but is not able to
> Then He is not omnipotent.
> If He is, but not willing
> Then He is malevolent.
> If He is both able and willing
> Then whence cometh evil?
> If He is neither able nor willing
> Then why call Him God?

The logic cannot be refuted. But it leaves an important question unanswered: What is the entire world about—the earth, sun, moon, stars, seas, mountains, humans and beasts? I admit I don't know and hence call myself an agnostic. I reject theism as well as atheism which answers this question with either a positive 'yes' or a positive 'no'.

India has a long and hallowed tradition of questioning the existence of God. Debiprasad Chattopadhyayay's *Indian Atheism: A Marxist Analysis* traces the questioning back to 6 century BC when Charvaka questioned both the existence of God and the sanctity of the Vedas. Later, Indian atheists questioned the Upanishads as well. Jainism and Buddhism put more emphasis on right thinking and right conduct than on the existence of God. It was evidently a society that was more open-minded and able to accept criticism than ours is today.

Since I have often questioned the existence of an omniscient (all-knowing), omnipotent (all-powerful), just and merciful God, I get a lot of letters from believers who denounce me as an ignorant, self-opinionated man, ever bent on mischief-making and provoking controversy. They quote religious texts, founders of religions, savants and scholars' theology to me. Most of these letters are in the form of assertions without reasons to back them up. I pity and envy them for having a blind faith that God exists.

Some time ago I received a longish article on the subject from T. Gopal Iyengar of Hyderabad. It made a lot of sense to me. He was logical, lucid and examined the subject from different angles. He spelt out his doubts and wrote to the sankaracharya of Kanchi and the head of the Ramakrishna Muth in Belur. From both of them he received terse replies brushing aside his queries and advising him to read this or that. Evidently they did not have the answers.

Iyengar starts by asserting that we are nurtured on religious beliefs from day one as we start imbibing our mother's milk.

By the time we are old enough to think for ourselves, we are thoroughly brainwashed into accepting the existence of God and are incapable of questioning it. The very few who ponder over the matter try to define God. How do you define someone or something you can't see, hear, touch or smell? Nevertheless, the feeling persists that there must be someone or some power that created the earth and life on it, and then takes it away, we know not where.

Two distinct approaches to the problem of defining God are available; the Hindic comprising Jain, Buddhist, Hindu and Sikh, and the Judaic (Jewish, Christian and Muslim). A good example of the Hindic approach is in the Vishnu Purana: 'O! Who can describe him who is not to be apprehended by the senses; who is the best of all things and the Supreme Soul, self-existent, who is devoid of all distinguishing characteristics of complexion, caste or the like, and is exempt from birth, vicissitude, death or decay; who is always alone; who exists everywhere and in whom all things here exist; and who is thence named Vasudev—the resplendent one in whom all things dwell.'

Right from the Vedic times to the advent of Sikhism, the pattern of the definition of God, with minor variations, has been the same. It should be noted that in none of them are justice, benevolence and mercy attributes of God as they are in Judaic religions where benevolence and mercy are important attributes of the Almighty. Indeed, in common Punjabi parlance, God is often described as 'vadda beparvaah'—the Great One who could not care less about human suffering.

That makes sense to me. Or how do you explain catastrophes like earthquakes and cyclones that take as heavy a toll on the innocent, upright and the God-fearing as they do on others? Why are so many children born blind, retarded or stricken with cancer? When there is so much injustice and cruelty in the world, why does the Almighty God not punish tyrants and the corrupt? Explanations like 'paying for deeds done in past lives' or 'punishments to be meted out in lives to come' have no provable rational basis and should be rejected.

So what is the answer? Iyengar does not give one. But from the way he argues I am inclined to conclude that we do not know whether or not God exists or ever existed. I go one step further and hold that his existence or non-existence is of no consequence to human beings.

Why do the innocent suffer? The question was put in different words by a Jewish rabbi whose only child was afflicted by terminal cancer. He and his wife were a god-fearing couple who had never harmed anyone. So why were they being punished by having their son taken away from them? The rabbi wrestled with the problem and put down his thoughts in a highly readable little book, *Why Bad Things Happen to Good People*. For inspiration he turned to the classic on the subject: the Book of Job in the Bible. I have read the Book of Job over and over again because it is beautifully worded but remain totally unconvinced with the arguments set out. Job was a good man without blemish. He was prosperous, had many sons, daughters, daughters-in-law and sons-in-law. Also, land, vineyards and herds of cattle. He was a man of conviction and believed that he owed his good fortune to God. Satan took on a bet with God that if Job was deprived of his family and possessions, he would lose his faith in God. Job assured himself, 'Whoever perished being innocent? Or where were the upright ever cut off? Even as I have seen those who plough iniquity and sow trouble reap the same… God will not cast away the blameless, nor will He uphold the evil-doers.'

Job lost everything: his children, lands, herds of cattle, and was himself afflicted with bodily sores and thrown out of his home. His wife pleaded with him, 'Curse God and die.' Three of his friends (Job's comforters) tried to argue him out of his faith. 'Man who is born of woman is of few days and full of trouble. He comes forth like a flower and fades away; he flees like a shadow and does not continue.' Job held fast to his faith but longed to present his case to God as his mouth was full of arguments. 'Great men are not always wise, nor do the aged always understand Justice.' God appeared before Job and reminded him that it was He who created everything on earth. He was all-knowing and all-powerful. God won the bet against Satan and Job was restored to good health and got back his family and property.

Does an unshakeable faith in God really explain why the innocent suffer? Not to me; it is no different from accepting what happens with good grace: Tera bhaanaa meetha laagey (What You [God] ordain tastes sweet). It does not. More often it leaves a bitter taste in the mouth and in the mind.

The fact of the matter is that we have as little comprehension of why the innocent suffer as we have of why the wicked prosper. Can anyone give rational answers to these questions without resorting to theories about karma, evil deeds committed in previous births, and punishments to come in lives hereafter? They are absolute hogwash, unworthy of consideration by people with serious minds.

One of the most cherished myths that mankind has clung to from time immemorial is that everyone pays for his misdeeds: as you sow, so shall you reap. People cite instances of individuals who acquired wealth by corrupt means, were later brought to book, or were afflicted with some incurable disease or their progeny turned out to be bad. For every such instance of an evil person paying for his sins, I could adduce twenty where they went unpunished. They did not suffer from pangs of guilt, remained in good health, ate well, lived well, enjoyed life and the esteem of their fellow citizens, sent their children to the best schools and colleges and saw them settled in plum jobs, married into rich families which ensured their future prospects. 'There is a just man who perishes in his righteousness, and a wicked man who prolongs life in his wickedness,' says the Bible.

When faced with hard evidence; that more often evil persons get a better deal in life than good people, upholders of the myth resort to inane explanations like 'honesty is its own reward', 'in the end, truth always triumphs'. They have even more devious explanations when confronted with cases of suffering inflicted on the good and the god-loving, such as their children being born blind, mentally deficient or spastic. 'It is karma. They are paying for the sins they committed in their past lives.' And they explain the prosperity of evil-doers with, 'They will surely pay for their sins in their lives to come: may they be reborn as snakes, pigs or vermin.' Such explanations are offered in the assurance that no one knows anything about past lives or the lives to come. As Ghalib said about paradise, I say about past and future lives: 'Dil kay behallaney ko yeh khayaal accha hai.' My friends don't suffer from the delusions that people suffer from for their misdeeds. How many paid the penalty for the crimes they had committed in November 1984? How many were punished for the

## RELIGION: A PERSONAL VIEW

destruction of the Babri Masjid? Far from being punished, three of them became members of Atal Bihari Vajpayee's Cabinet, and the man who soured the wind by his mischievously conceived rath yatra from Somnath to Ayodhya and spread the whirlwind of communal violence, which has not abated to this day, was once the man-in-waiting to be the next prime minister. Do J. Jayalalithaa and Laloo Prasad Yadav feel guilty for squandering public money on weddings in their families? Do stockbrokers who fiddled with public money to the tune of thousands of crores, Pandit Sukh Ram or Ravi Sidhu, have sleepless nights for what they did?

I don't think so. They must have explanations which give them peace. No, my friends, there is no justice in the world. To succeed in life you have to be the three Cs (or chalakis in Hindi): chaalak (cunning), chaaploos (sycophant) and chaar-sau-bees (a cheat as defined under Section 420 of the Indian Penal Code).

God has no place in Jain theology. Instead, Jains believe in 'enlightened' human beings because escape is only possible in human form. Jains also reject the Vedas, the priestly order of the Brahmins and the caste system.

The Jain influence in India is largely due to the comparative affluence of the community. Some of India's biggest industrial houses are Jain—Dalmia, Sarabhai, Walchand, Kasturbhai Lalbhai, Sahu Jain. The proportion of literacy among them is also high. Mahatma Gandhi, who was greatly influenced by the doctrine of ahimsa (non-violence), elevated it from a personal and ethical creed to a programme of national and political policy.

Despite ten years in Delhi's Modern School, an institution founded by the Jain family of Lala Sultan Singh, his son, Raghubir Singh, and currently controlled by Raghubir Singh's son, General Virendra Singh, I knew nothing about the Jain faith. Even in college I had some friends who were Jains, but I never got to know anything about their religious beliefs except that they were strict vegetarians. I also learnt that Mahatma Gandhi was profoundly influenced by Jain tenets, and the Jains were among the richest in our country. Also, their temples are among the most beautiful in India.

It was only in the 'sixties, when I had to teach a course on comparative religion at Princeton University, and later at Swarthmore College and the University of Hawaii, that I read books on Jainism in order to pass on the information to my American students. I was deeply impressed with what I learnt. I admitted if I had to choose a religion to subscribe to, it would be Jainism. It came closest to agnosticism and the code of ethics to which, as a rationalist, I subscribed.

In the 'seventies, when I was the editor of the *Illustrated Weekly of India*, then the largest and the most influential weekly journal in the country, I wrote to the chief ministers of all the states that if they imposed a blanket ban on shikar in their states in honour of Jain Mahavira, I would give them all the publicity they wanted. Eight chief ministers responded to my appeal and banned killing for sport. I might mention that at the time, the Jains who owned the Times of India group of papers, including the *Illustrated Weekly of India,* had been deprived of control of the company and it was run by the government. The Jains had nothing to do with my anti-shikar crusade. As a matter of fact, when the Jains regained control of the Times of India group, they sacked me.

The word 'jain' is derived from 'jina', one who has conquered himself. Jains believe that their religious system was evolved by twenty-four tirthankaras (or makers of the river crossing), three of whom, Rhishabha, Ajitnath and Aristanemi, systematized their religious doctrines. Most of the Jain hagiography is legendary. But we do have reliable historical evidence of the existence of Parshvanath (877-777 BC), the twenty-third tirthankara, and Mahavira, the twenty-fourth (599-527 BC). There is reason to believe that in its formative phase, Jainism was a reaction against Brahminical Hindusim.

Vardhamana Mahavira was born in 599 BC in

Kundagrama, a town north of Patna. He was the second son of a nobleman and was reared in the lap of luxury. The Jains love to enumerate everything. According to them, the child Mahavira was cared for by five nurses and enjoyed five kinds of joy. When he came of age, he was married and his wife bore him a daughter. But neither his wife, nor his child, nor the affairs of the state occupied his mind. On the death of his parents (according to one version, by suicide), he took the permission of his elder brother to retire to the jungles. He was then thirty years old. For twelve years he fasted and meditated 'in a squatting position, with joined heels, exposing himself to the heat of the sun, with knees high and the head low, in deep meditation'. In the midst of abstract meditation, he reached kevala (total) omniscience. He became nirgrantha—without ties or knots.

Mahavira discarded his clothes and spent the next thirty years of his life wandering from place to place. He spoke to no one, never stayed anywhere for more than one night, ate only raw food and strained the water he drank. He allowed vermin to feed on his body and carried a broom to sweep insects away from his path lest he trod on them. People scoffed at him and often tormented him. But he never said anything to them. He died in 527 BC, or, as the Jains put it, at the age of seventy-two, he cut asunder the ties of birth, old age and death.

## RELIGION: A PERSONAL VIEW

Everything, animate or inanimate, has jiva (life-force). No one has the right to take another's life. The way of deliverance, said Mahavira, is in the pursuit of three gems (tri-b-atans): right faith, right knowledge and right conduct. Right conduct prescribes five principles: sanctity of life (non-violence is the supreme law); truthfulness; respect for property; chastity and abandonment of worldly possessions.

Religions have had a renaissance in the form of belief in the irrational and kowtowing to superstitions. It is not a subject to be dismissed as a matter of academic irrelevance. What faith can you impose on a party that ruled us for six years and is the most important element in the Opposition when it changes the entrance to its office from one side to the other because a Vaastu expert advises it that that would bring it better luck? And what do you think of an otherwise acceptable leader who wants the number of the house allotted to him to be changed from number 8 to 6A because the former is inauspicious? Or a Jayalalithaa and a Shobhaa Dé adding another 'a' to their first names because they believe it will improve their fortunes?

People who watch games on their TV sets must have noticed how many players attribute their achievements to God who, they presume, lives up in the clouds. Tendulkar, Ganguly, Dravid, Laxman and other batsmen, as soon as they score fifty, 100, 150 or 200 runs, first take off their helmets to raise their bats in order to acknowledge the cheering of spectators, then look briefly upwards to give thanks to the ooperwala. And this is not only the case with cricket players. Before the start of a hockey match, you will notice rival teams huddle together at either end of the field, put their heads together and say a short prayer for victory. Likewise, tennis players like the Amritraj brothers and Leander Paes may be noticed kissing the crucifix they wear around their neck to lend more punch to their services and smashes. I've noticed players of some other nations perform similar gestures in honour of their deities: Pakistanis, Sri Lankans, Africans and Latinos. I have never seen Englishmen, Australians, New Zealanders or white Africans take much notice of the God of Sports. And in one interview in *Savaal Aapkey*, cricket celebrity Harbhajan Singh parried all the flattering comments hurled at him by attributing his success to bhagwan.

Nor I do think going on a pilgrimage makes one a better person. On my TV set, I've watched pilgrims gather in Jerusalem and Bethlehem, at Bodh Gaya, Prayag and Haridwar, at Mecca and Medina, at Amritsar, Hemkunt and Patna. I have met people who had been on pilgrimages; they looked very pleased with themselves. But I did not notice any changes for the better in them. If they were prone to lying, cheating, backbiting, scandal-mongering, using bad language before they left for their holy cities or rivers, they came back and resumed lying, cheating, backbiting, scandal-mongering and using bad language.

Truly had Guru Nanak spoken: Ath sath teerath nahaaie utrey nahee maeil (You may bathe at the sixty-eight places of pilgrimage, it will not wash the dirt off your body [and mind]). That does not deter the Guru's followers from doing precisely what he had castigated as a useless practice, or from going to pilgrim centres.

Some years ago, a film called *Nanak Naam Jahaaz* (the Holy Name is a ship that will take you across the waters of life) was shown in cinemas across northern India. Its theme was a man blinded in an accident visiting gurdwaras all over India. When he came to the sanctum of the temple and restored his vision, hundreds of thousands of people saw the film and were convinced that it was the truth, when in their hearts they knew it was a lie.

The Kumbh Mela at Allahabad is a pilgrimage on a scale grander than any ever seen in the world; as if the entire population of a country the size of Australia was packed into a few square miles of land surrounding the sangam (confluence) of three rivers; two, the Ganga and the Yamuna, are real; the third, Saraswati, mythical. The bandobast required to organize road, rail and air transport, housing, feeding, sanitation and maintaining law and order boggles the mind. One small mishap and the consequences would be disastrous. Is it worth taking such risks?

The people who go to the mela certainly think so. It is always a never-to-be-forgotten spectacle of sight and sound: thousands of ash-smeared Naga sadhus marching in processions from their ashrams and encampments to plunge into the waters of the Ganga and the Yamuna, hundreds of pandals with saffron-clad swamis chanting mantras or expounding the essential tenets of dharma.

And what about prayer? I was a child of about four living in a tiny village with my grandmother; she taught me my first prayer. I was scared of the dark and prone to having nightmares. She told me that whenever I was frightened, I should recite the following lines by Guru Arjan:

> Taatee vau na laagaee, peer-Brahma saranaee
> Chowgird hamaarey Raam-kar, dukh lagey na bhaee
>
> (No ill-winds touch you, the great lord your protector be
> Around you Lord Rama has drawn a protective line.
> Brother, no harm will come to thee.)

Being young, innocent and having infinite trust in my granny's assurances of the efficacy of these lines, I found they worked like magic. Later, I discovered that most Sikh children were taught the same lines even before they learnt other prayers. The hymn had four more lines:

> Satgur poora bhetiya
> Jis banat banaaee Raam naam aukhad deeya.

> Eka liv laayee Raakh liye tin raakhan har, sabh biaadh mitaayee
> Kaho Nanak kirpa bhaee, Prabhu bhaye Sahaaee
>
> (The true guru was revealed in his fullness, the one who did all create
> He gave the name of Rama as medicine, in Him alone I repose my faith.
> He saves all who deserve to be saved, He removes all worries of the mind.
> Sayeth Nanak, God became my helper, He was kind.)

Mark the Hindu terminology in this short prayer: Peer, Brahma, Raam-kaar, Raam-naam, and Prabhu. As a matter of fact, a painstaking scholar counted the number of times the name of God appears in the Adi Granth. The total comes to around 16,000. Of these over 14,000 are of Hindu origin: Hari, Ram, Govind, Narayan, Krishna, Murari, Madhav, Vithal and so on. There are also a sizeable number of Islamic origin: Allah, Rehman, Rahim, Kareem and so on. The Sikh term 'Wahe Guru' appears only sixteen times.

All religions borrow a lot from the others with which they come into contact; there is not a single religion in the world that has not borrowed some concept or the other from another: some borrow vocabulary and even rituals. In the Judaic family of religions—Judaism, Christianity and Islam—there is plenty of evidence of wholesale borrowing. A good example is Islam. Its monotheism also exists in Judaism and Christianity. Its five daily prayers have roughly the same names as those of Jews; its greeting 'salaam aalaikum' is a variation of the Jewish 'shalom alekh'; turning to Mecca for namaaz is based on the Jews turning to Jerusalem; their food inhibitions (regarding pig's meat as unclean; halaal is the same as the Jewish kosher), the custom of circumcising male children (sunnat) is also Jewish.

There is a lot of emphasis on what one should eat or drink in our religious traditions which has neither logic nor any bearing on health. For some beef is forbidden but pig meat is okay; in other beef is okay but pig meat is haraam (forbidden). Some insist that animals meant to be eaten must be beheaded at one stroke (jhatka); others insist they should be bled to death before they can be certified as edible (halaal). Vegetarians have kitchen fads of their own: some will not eat vegetables like onions, garlic, carrots or radishes because they are polluted by contact with the soil. But even they make an exception in the case of potatoes. How can anyone relish a vegetarian meal without spuds?

A couple of weeks ago I learnt of another eccentricity. The wife and daughter of a senior Bengali IAF officer told me that in Bengali homes no chicken or chicken eggs are eaten: they prefer to eat duck and duck eggs. I asked them why? Their answer was amusing. Because, they said, Muslims relish chicken, so Hindus decided that eating chickens was un-Hindu. By that logic Bengali Hindus should be consuming ham and bacon which Muslims abominate.

Among Punjabis the kitchen fads are equally mind-boggling. Though both Hindus and Sikhs strictly abstain from eating beef (the Namdhari sect of Sikhs gained popularity for murdering Muslim cow butchers, and were later blown up by cannons to be acclaimed as martyrs), there is little enthusiasm for eating pig meat. At the most they take pickled pork (achaar), preferably made of wild boar meat. Ham and bacon, introduced to India by the English, can only be seen on the tables of the westernized Punjabis. And far from not eating chicken because it is relished by Muslims, chicken is the non-vegetarian Punjabi's favourite food. Chicken tandoori is the Punjabis' national bird.

Religious people who like to drink do so no matter what their scriptures say against drinking alcohol. On the contrary, taking wine is a part of Catholic and Anglican religious ritual. Only later sects like the Mormons who practice polygamy, the Jehovah's Witnesses, the Christian Scientists, the Quakers and the Plymouth Brethren disapproved of imbibing liquor. There are lots of references to the joys of drinking in the Old Testament.

The attitude towards drinking underwent a change with the advent of Islam. Scholars still disagree over whether the Quran forbids it as haraam (unlawful) or only censures it as something undesirable. So drinking in public is forbidden in most Muslim countries except Turkey, Tunisia, Algeria and Egypt, which are comparatively westernized. In the more conservative Muslim countries like Sudan, Iraq, Iran, Afghanistan, Pakistan and Bangladesh, despite prohibition, people manage to get alcohol.

The Hindic family of religions—Hinduism, Jainism, Buddhism and Sikhism—took a more tolerant view of drinking. Our gods drank somras; on many religious festivals drinking hard liquor or bhang (hashish) is de rigueur. My Sikh friends who disapprove of my drinking quote passages from the Granth Sahib to prove drinking is forbidden by the Sikh faith. Nevertheless, next to the Parsis (Zoroastrianism does not forbid drinking), the Sikhs are the biggest tipplers in India. The strong disapproval of drinking is a later development among certain Hindu reformist movements and was given religious sanction by men like Mahatma Gandhi and Morarji Desai.

The intermingling of faiths is much more in evidence in the Hindic family of religions: Hinduism, Jainism, Buddhism and Sikhism. All share a belief in karma, the cycle of birth-death-rebirth, meditation and so on. Needless to say, they also share much of their religious terminology.

## RELIGION: A PERSONAL VIEW

Since Sikhism was the last of these major religions to emerge and the only one to come in contact with Islam, it is the only one which, coming in contact with the Bhakti cult, took a lot of the terminology of Islam from the sufi saints. When the thekedars (contractors or purveyors) of religion claim that their faith owes nothing to others and is therefore the purest of the pure, they make me laugh at their ignorance.

But to come back to prayer, I have memorized the principal power mantras of Hindus, Christians, Muslims and Sikhs but have not been able to work out why the followers of these religions endow them with powers above other mantras. It is generally agreed by all Hindus that the Gayatri Mantra is regarded as the most powerful invocation. I have translated it into English and often recited it while half asleep lest it escape my memory. I also know passages from the Gita and the Upanishads by rote which read as well but are relegated to secondary importance because the Gayatri Mantra is the mahamantra.

If the most popular shabad among Sikhs is the one my grandmother taught me, for Christians, it is the twenty-third psalm:

> The Lord is my shepherd; I shall not want. He maketh me to lie down in green pastures. He leadeth me beside the still waters. He restoreth my soul; He leadeth me in

paths of righteousness for his name's sake. Yea, though I walk through the valley of the shadow of death, I will fear no evil; for thou art with me, thy rod and thy staff they comfort me.

The two most popular verses of the Quran that appear in Muslim mausoleums, including the Taj Mahal, are Sura Yaseen (which festoons the entrance gate) and Ayat-ul-Kursi, the throne verse. Of the two, Ayat-ul-Kursi is the more popular. Many Muslims wear it in their amulets. I have one in bidri and silver on my wall. I got a gold medallion from Tehran which my daughter, Mala, and then her daughter, Naina, wore in their necklaces while taking their examinations. Neither knew what it meant but felt reassured because their Muslim friends told them it was very powerful. It was as follows:

> There is no God but Allah, the living, the self-subsisting, the eternal. No slumber or sleep can seize Him. His are all the things in heaven and on earth. Who can intercede in His presence except as He permits? He knows the past, the present and the future. He cares equally for all. He in his knowledge grades his creations. His kingdom extends over the heaven and the earth. He is the guardian, He is the Preserver. He is the highest. He is Supreme.

I am far from being a devout Sikh. But the first thing that I did when I set out to write about the religion and history of the Sikhs was to translate the Japji, the Sikhs' morning prayer. It was the earliest translation of the morning prayer rendered by a Sikh to be published abroad. Even while working on the translation, my literary inspiration was the Bible whose language I believe is most suited for the translation of scriptures of other religions.

> There is one God.
> He is the supreme truth.
> He, The Creator.
> Is without fear and without hate.
> He, The Omnipresent,
> Pervades the universe.
> He is not born,
> Nor does He die to be born again.
> By His grace
> shalt thou worship Him.
> Before time itself
> There was truth.
> When time began to run its course
> He was the truth.
> Even now, He is the truth
> And
> Evermore shall truth prevail.
> Not by thought alone, can He be known
> Though one think,
> A hundred thousand times;
> Not in solemn silence

> Not in deep meditation.
> Though fasting yields an abundance of virtue
> It cannot appease the hunger for truth.
> No, by none of these,
> Nor by a hundred thousand other devices,
> Can God be reached.
> How then shall the Truth be known? How the veil of false illusion torn?
> O Nanak, thus runneth the writ divine,
> The righteous path—let it be Thine.

No doubt, it's the simplest vocabulary, unambiguous and well-worded. I know many other passages in the Quran which read as well but I have not understood why the throne verse is endowed with more power than the others.

The importance of the Japji for the Sikhs cannot be overstated. Besides being the morning prayer to be recited at amritvela (the pre-dawn ambrosial hour), it forms the opening statement of the Sikhs' scripture, the Granth Sahib, and is regarded as the essence of Sikh theology.

We are not certain about the time when it was composed, but inner evidence points to the conclusion that it was in the later years of the Guru's life and he took several days to finalize it.

It is the only piece in the Granth Sahib that can be read as one sustained piece, where the Guru spells out his vision of God as the ultimate, timeless truth and the path a seeker must take in order to achieve salvation. He was evidently inspired by the Upanishads: many theologians subscribe to the view that Sikhism is the essence of Vedanta.

The Japji is the only part of the Granth Sahib that is meant to be recited, preferably in silent meditation and not set to the ragas of classical music like the other nearly 6,000 hymns of the Granth Sahib. The compiler, the fifth guru, Arjan, gave it the first place as it contained everything that is cardinal to Sikhism.

The founder of Sikhism, Guru Nanak, was born in 1469 to Hindu parents in a village north-west of Lahore, now in Pakistan. He was a wayward child who spent a lot of time talking to itinerant holy men. In his mid-twenties he left home with a Muslim family retainer and minstrel. They visited Hindu places of pilgrimage along the Ganges, went south to Sri Lanka and then west to Mecca and Medina. Nanak carried a notebook in which he wrote hymns in praise of God and set down his dialogues with men of religious learning.

There are not many references to historical events in Nanak's writings, but he does mention the invasion of northern India by the Mughal conqueror Babur in 1526 and the havoc it caused. Nanak was imprisoned for some time. He acquired a sizable following among both Hindus and Muslims. When he died in 1539 there was a dispute among his followers: the Muslims wanted to bury him because they thought he was one of them; the Hindus wanted to cremate him in the belief that he remained a Hindu to the end.

Nanak's teachings were a blend of Hinduism and Islam. He rejected Hindu polytheism and idol worship and accepted Islamic monotheism. He rejected the Hindu caste system and asceticism. 'Be in the world but not worldly,' he said. He emphasized the duty to work and earn a living.

It is clear that Nanak wished to set up a community apart from Hindus and Muslims. He appointed his closest disciple as the second guru, and the second guru appointed his closest disciple to be the third. Thereafter succession remained restricted to one family. The fourth guru founded the city of Amritsar in 1574. His son, Guru Arjan, raised the Harmandir (the temple of God) in the city. Later rebuilt in marble and covered with gold leaf, it became the Sikhs' most important place of pilgrimage.

Guru Arjan complied the Granth Sahib, the sacred scripture of the Sikhs. It comprises more than 6,000 hymns, all meant to be sung to the tune of the different ragas of Indian classical music. Besides presenting the writings of the gurus, it includes the compositions of Hindu and Muslim saints.

By Guru Arjan's time the Sikhs had become a sizable community, which alarmed the Muslim rulers. Arjan was summoned to Lahore where, after days of torture, he died. The same fate met the ninth guru, who was arrested, brought to Delhi and executed in 1675.

His only son, Gobind Rai, took up arms in defence of the community. 'Where all other means have failed, it is righteous to draw the sword out of its scabbard,' he wrote to the Mughal emperor. He called the Sikhs to gather at Anandpur and baptized five into a new fraternity called the Khalsa, or the pure. They vowed never to cut their hair or beards and always to carry a sword. He gave them a common surname—Singh, or Lion—and changed his own name to Gobind Singh.

Gobind Singh fought Hindu rajas and Muslim Mogul armies. He lost all four of his sons and was assassinated by two of his Muslim retainers. The Punjabi peasantry eventually rose and ousted the Muslim rule in northern India. This paved the way for a Sikh kingdom under Ranjit Singh, who ruled over Punjab until 1839.

The Sikh history is a long saga of bloody conflicts with the Muslims. When the British partitioned the region, almost half the Sikh population found itself in Pakistan. The Muslims drove them into India, killing hundreds of thousands. In their turn, the Sikhs drove the Muslims out of towns and villages in northern India with as much slaughter. How ironic that Sikhs should be confused with Muslims in the aftermath of 9/11!

Having spent the best part of my life working on Sikh history and translating selected passages of the Gurbani, I felt I owed it to myself to read the Granth Sahib. Many questions rose in my mind. Knowing the bigoted, unintelligent approach of the self-appointed custodians of matters scriptural, I will not start a public debate. But there are some historical and linguistic aspects of the Gurbani that need elucidation. To start with, I would like scholars to compare the hymns of Kabir and Namdeo as they appear in the Granth Sahib with those in Hindi and Marathi. How did they travel from Varanasi and Maharashtra to Amritsar where the fifth Sikh Guru, Arjan, compiled the scriptures? Kabir's dohas in Hindi are different from his language in the Granth Sahib. How could he have composed the acrostics based on Gurumukhi at a time when the alphabet had yet to be finalized?

The case of Namdeo's baani is equally puzzling. I recall the late P.N. Oak, then secretary to the information and broadcasting ministry, asking me to give him Namdeo's baani in the Granth Sahib. Oak was a Maharashtrian studying the writings of Maharashtrian saint-poets. He went through the material and said: 'It is Namdeo but the vocabulary is different.' Did Guru Arjan rewrite both Kabir's and Namdeo's works before incorporating them in his compilation?

That reminds me of another work whose origin still intrigues me. Some years ago I translated Bapu Gandhi's favourite hymn, 'Vaishnavjan to tainay kahiye', said to be the compilation of Narsi Mehta who lived in the nineteenth century. When my translation was published, Swaran Singh, the editor of the *Sikh Review* in Calcutta, drew my attention to one of Guru Arjan's hymns on which Narsi Mehta's was based word for word. It could not have been a mere coincidence that Mehta had the same message for humanity that the Guru gave almost three centuries earlier.

There are things in our scriptures which we accept as the gospel truth without ever questioning their veracity. Two such truisms are 'the truth always triumphs' (Satyameva Jayate) and 'honesty is the best policy'. There are good reasons for accepting them at face value but when I begin to ponder over them, I begin to wonder how much of it is wishful make-believe and how much of it proven reality. I concede that truth should always prevail and honesty should be the best policy, but is it, in fact, so?

The scriptures answer the question in the affirmative. 'Great is Truth, and mighty above all things,' says the Bible (Apocrypha 4:41). It might be recalled that the words are taken from Esdras, which tells the story of King Darius of Persia who asked three young Jewish scholars: What is the strongest thing in the world? The first one replied that it was wine, the second said the king was the strongest, the third said women were strongest and added a postscript: 'But above all things, truth beareth away the victory.' It became an article of faith, its Latin form being 'Magna est veritas, et praevalebit (Great is truth and it prevails)'. Its shortened form MVP was often used as a motto on the flags and shields of countries claiming that they were fighting for the truth.

Guru Nanak equated truth with God. So did Mahatma Gandhi. Nanak put truthful conduct on an even higher pedestal:

> Sachhon orey sab ko
> Osper sachh aachaar.
>
> (Truth above all
> Above truth, truthful conduct.)

Gandhi went along with the guru in as much as he also made truthful conduct the central principle of his life. It should be evident that regarding honesty to be the best policy is a part and parcel of his concept of truthful conduct. 'To think good thoughts is one thing, to act upon them is another,' he wrote.

So convinced are we with such truisms that we also believe that anyone who transgresses the moral code pays a heavy price. Haraam ki kamaayi kabhi hazam nahin hoti (what is earned illicitly can never be digested). As a matter of fact we all know a lot of people who live very well with illicit earnings and do not have problems with their digestion. They also do not suffer from insomnia. I know a few contemporaries who lied about their educational achievements, claimed that they had a first or higher second division, when actually they had thirds, did well in their interviews, landed good jobs and retired on fat pensions. No indigestion, no insomnia; they lived in good health into their eighties, respected by those not aware of the untruthful beginnings and envied by those who did. We have innumerable cases of wanton murders and deaths caused by drunken drivers where the culprits have got away by bribing eyewitnesses to retract their statements and tell lies under oath. Now turn your critical eye on your own lawmakers—MPs and MLAs. How many of them are 'tainted' (the word includes cheating, incitement to violence and murder)? They may not all be respected but their success in life cannot be denied. So what exactly does Satyameva Jayate mean?

According to our ancient scriptures, both Hindu and Sikh, krodh (anger) is as serious a shortcoming as kama (lust), lobh (greed), moh (self-love) and ahankaar (arrogance). They exhort us to overcome them in order to achieve moksha (salvation). They do not tell us how to go about getting the better of them. As far as anger is concerned, people have their own formulae: 'when roused to anger, count to ten before answering' or 'swallow the insult and keep your mouth shut'. There is no doubt that a person who loses his cool loses the argument. Another school of thought is that it is better to let off steam and get it over with because if you contain your anger, your blood pressure will rise and you may get peptic ulcers. I have evolved my own formula to get anger out of my system. I say nothing to the person who has insulted or snubbed me but when I narrate the incident to my friends later, I let loose a torrent of the choicest abuse in Punjabi and Hindustani—I have a large repertoire of filthy words in four languages—and purge myself of my anger. I even feel exhilarated for having scored over my traducer by saying nothing to him or her and I cleanse my system by letting out all the accumulated venom in front of third parties who thoroughly enjoy my outburst.

For many years, when I was young and believed in resolutions to improve myself, my New Year's resolve used to be to not run people down behind their backs. I was in the habit of doing so and hated myself afterwards. Whatever I said somehow reached the ears of the person I had maligned. When confronted by him or her, I had to deny what I had said and had reason to feel low in my self-estimation. I was able to check myself from indulging in vilifying people behind their backs for a few days. I resumed the bad habit, but somehow it got less and less on its own. I came to realize the truth of Guru Nanak's admonition:

## RELIGION: A PERSONAL VIEW

Nanak, phikka boleeai
Tan man plukka hoi.

(Nanak, if you speak ill of the people
Your body and mind will fall sick.)

The Guru's words can also be interpreted as applying when saying nasty things to people to their faces. Many people make it a point to say hurtful things to others and justify their doing so. When in return they get more than they gave, there is a slanging match in which both participants get hurt while others enjoy the spectacle.

As for forgiveness, all religions counsel it. My father had a short temper; his father was even more ill-tempered. His pet word for me was bharwah (pimp) and since I went to a school that had lady teachers, rann mureed—disciple of a slut. My father never used bad language but being overworked, he was impatient and inclined to snap at everyone. We were terrified of him and kept out of his way as much as we could. In the later years of his life, he mellowed a great deal and I looked forward to joining him in the evenings for a sundowner. However, I could never get over my allergy towards people with short tempers. Incidents of people snubbing me still rankle in my mind. I have no forgiveness. Once somebody loses his temper with me, I write them off forever and no amount of their trying to make amends makes any difference in my attitude towards them.

## ON RELIGION

In his own way Guru Nanak was also regarded as the dispeller of the darkness of ignorance, superstition and hate and the prophet of light and understanding among people.

The theologian, Bhai Gurdas, described Nanak's achievements in the following words:

> The true guru, Nanak, was then born;
> Fog and mist evaporated
> And light shone on the earth.
> As the rising sun dispels the dark and outshines the stars,
> As flee the herd of deer when a lion roars
> Without pause, without turning back for assurance.
> So fled evil from the world.

Nanak believed that the ideal was to achieve godliness while performing one's worldly tasks—raaj mein jog, that is, without renouncing the world or turning into an ascetic.

> Religion lieth not in the patched coat the Yogi wears,
> Not in the staff he bears,
> Nor in the ashes on his body.
> Religion lieth not in rings in the ears,
> Not in a shaven head,
> If thou must the path of true religion see
> Among the world's impurities, be of impurities free.

And again:

> The lotus in the water is not wet
> Nor the water-fowl in the stream.

## RELIGION: A PERSONAL VIEW

> If a man would live, but by the world untouched,
> Meditate and repeat the name of the lord Supreme.

Nanak preached a crusade against meaningless superstition. During his time (and even today) the higher castes attached exaggerated respect to the sanctity of the kitchen: who may enter it, who may cook, what kind of food is pure and what is polluted. He wrote:

> There are worms in wood and cowdung cakes,
> There is life in the corn ground into bread.
> There is life in the water which makes it green.
> How then be clean when impurity is over the kitchen
>     spread?
> Impurity of the heart is greed, of tongue, untruth,
> Impurity of the eye is coveting another's wealth,
>     his wife, her comeliness.
> Impurity of the ears is listening to calumny.

He believed in the cleansing and purging qualities of prayer, naam. In the morning prayer, Japji, he wrote:

> As hands or feet besmirched with slime,
> Water washes white;
> As garments dark with grime,
> Rinsed with soap are made light;
> So when sin soils the soul
> The Name alone shall make it whole;
> Words do not the saint or sinner make.
> Action alone is written in the book of fate.

What we sow that alone we take;
O Nanak, be saved or forever transmigrate.

Nanak equated God with truth. Truth is not an academic concept but something that has to become a principle of living. Guru Nanak was more conscious of nature than the gurus who succeeded him. His baramasi has some beautiful descriptions of natural phenomena. The chirping of sparrows at the break of dawn, the drone of cicadas in forest glades and, of course, black clouds, thunder, lightning and rain during the monsoon. I give one example: 'Mori runjhun laya, bhainey savan aya' (Raga Vadhans):

> Sweet sound of water gurgling down the water-spout
> (The peacock's shrill, exultant cry)
> Sister, it's Savan, the month of rain!
> Beloved—thine eyes bind me in a spell
> (they pierce through me like daggers)
> They fill my heart with greed and longing;
> For one glimpse of thee I'll give my life
> For thy name may I be a sacrifice.
> When thou art mine, my heart fills with pride,
> What can I be proud of if thou art not with me?
> Woman, smash thy bangles on thy bedstead
> Break thy arms, break the arms of thy couch;
> Thy adornments hold no charms
> The Lord is in another's arms.
> The Lord liked not thy bangle-seller
> Thy bracelets and glass bangles.

## RELIGION: A PERSONAL VIEW

He doth spurn
Arms that do not the Lord's neck embrace
With anguish shall forever burn.
All my friends have gone to their lovers
I feel wretched, whose door shall I seek?
Friends, of proven virtue and fair am I
Lord, does nothing about me find favour in Thine eyes?
I plaited my tresses,
With vermilion daubed the parting of my hair
And went to Him
But with me He would not lie.
My heart is grief-stricken, I could die.
I wept, and the world wept with me.
Even birds of the forest cried,
Only my soul torn out of my body shed not a! tear,
Nay, my soul which separated me from my beloved
    shed not a tear
In a dream He came to me
(I woke), and He was gone.

Prabhat pheris—going around singing in the early hours of the dawn—are customary at Hindu and Sikh religious festivals in the plains of northern India. Behind the block of flats where I live, there is a small gurdwara. A week or so before the birth anniversary of Guru Nanak a loud cracker is exploded in the gurdwara courtyard at 4 a.m. We are rudely shaken out of our slumber; most doze off again. About a dozen men and women assemble in the gurdwara and form a procession. The only music accompaniments are the chimta and the dholak (drum). They go around the block singing Bhai Gurdas's eulogy, 'Satgur Nanak pragatya, mitti dhund jag chaanan hoya (The true Guru Nanak made his appearance; dust and mist evaporated from the face of the earth).' This is followed by some hymns composed by the guru. The singing is not very melodious, but it is a manifestation of the singers' faith in their guru.

One prabhat pheri that still haunts me was the one I heard on my first day in Santiniketan in 1933. The monsoon was in full swing. From the window of the train to Bolpur, it was a vast expanse of water on both sides. 'Shamudro—it is like the sea,' remarked the ticket collector, who happened to be the only other person in the compartment. The Bolpur Railway Station looked drenched and desolate. I asked the station master how I could get to Santiniketan. 'Take a jutka,' he said.

I did not know what a jutka was. I found a small bullock-cart with a thatched roof, asked the owner if he could take me to Santiniketan. 'Baitho,' he replied, 'do taaka' (two rupees). I hopped in. We drove through a flooded countryside.

He dropped me off at the office. I was expected. I signed the entry register and was conducted to a room I was to share with a Buddhist bhikhu from Sri Lanka. Then

## RELIGION: A PERSONAL VIEW

I was taken to the dining hall where I had a plateful of rice and maachher jhole (fish curry). I got to my room and made acquaintance with my roommate. The room had no furniture of any kind. The bhikhu had a hurricane lamp by his pillow and read late into the night. I spread my bedding roll at the other end of the room. I had never slept on a hard cement floor. I was tired and dozed off before Bhikhu Manjushri blew out the hurricane lantern.

I slept fitfully, uncertain about what I had let myself in for. I must have fallen asleep because I began to dream. I heard the voices of an angelic choir at a distance, coming towards me. I realized I was not dreaming; it was for real. I groped my way in the dark and opened the door. The soft moonlight of the waning moon filtered through the mist of a gentle drizzle. I saw a dozen boys and girls dressed in white, carrying lanterns and candles, walking in a procession, singing as they went around the campus. Later I learnt it was the varsha mangal (the welcoming of the rains).

I envy other people's faith and religious fervour. I regret I will forever remain an outsider, sceptical of all pilgrimages save the one in one's own heart.

To quote Fitzgerald:

> ...Pilgrim, pilgrimage and Road
> was but myself towards myself, and your
> Arrival but myself, at my door.

Came, you lost atoms to your
Centre draw
Rays that have wandered into darkness wide
Return, and back into your Sun subside.

In the days left to me, I have come to the conclusion that I've been an imposter all my life. I have written several books on the religion and the history of the Sikhs, published translations of selected hymns from the Gurbani without having ever read the Guru Granth Sahib from cover to cover. Nevertheless, when people refer to me as a scholar of Sikhism, I protest so mildly that they think I am being modest.

I am now trying to fill up the gaps in my knowledge by devoting my entire summer vacation to reading the Guru Granth Sahib in the morning; I devote my afternoons to reading Urdu poets, from Meer and Ghalib to Faiz Ahmed Faiz, Kaifi Azmi, Javed Akhtar and others. So the mornings are devoted to reading about praises of the Lord, the importance of the Guru for spiritual elevation, the need to conquer lust, anger, desire and arrogance by squashing one's ego and renouncing wine and women. The afternoons are spent reading about the joy that drinking liquor, making love to women and boys with rosy cheeks and rounded bottoms provide.

In short, it is the temple in the a.m., the tavern after p.m. I have become a split personality. By the time my vacation is over, I would have finished my first complete reading of the Guru Granth Sahib. I would have also gone through the diwans of Urdu classical masters and modern poets. I fear I will end up as a schizophrenic in need of psychiatric help.

I comfort myself by believing that Mirza Asadullah Khan Ghalib must have faced the same dilemma. His Muslim friends who followed the Shariat law strictly must have chided him for not saying his prayers regularly and for his indulgence in wine. A man who had known want, woe and fear, a man who begged for a pittance from the king, I wonder, how he could decide so quickly to change his ways and give up drinking.

To wit:

> So have I lived and passed my days
> How can I bring myself to say that God exists.
> God the Bounteous Giver,
> God the Beneficent?
> For God's possible for those who lead happy
>     sheltered lives,
> And know God's grace and His loving care.

Sauda, another great master of Urdu verse, was even more outspoken about the joys of drinking:

> Saaqi gayee bahaar, dil mim rahee havas
> Too minnaton sayjaam dey
> Aur main kahoon kay 'bas'.

(O Saki, gone is the spring of youth,
Remains but one regret in this heart of mine
That thou has never pressed the goblet in my hand,
And I protested 'I've had enough wine'.)

By the time the day is over and I turn indoors for my sundowner, I am a thoroughly confused person. I pour myself a hefty slug of Scotch 'n' soda and put on my cassette player. I refrain from putting on kirtan in respect for people who would consider it a sacrilege and instead listen to Bach, Beethoven or Mozart. I come to the comforting conclusion: 'imposter' is too strong a word for me, but 'humbug' fits me to a tee.

# A GOOD LIFE IS THE ONLY TRUE RELIGION

George Bernard Shaw once wrote that every intelligent man makes his own religion, though there are a hundred versions of it. Evolving a personal religion for myself has been a lifelong quest. It has been as the renowned poet Allama Mohammad Iqbal put it:

> Dhoondta phirta hoon main, ai Iqbal, apney aap ko
> Aap hee goya musaafir, aap hee manzil hoon main.
>
> (O Iqbal, I go about everywhere looking for myself
> As if I were the wayfarer as well as the destination.)

I was born a Sikh and reared in Sikhism. My parents were orthodox Sikhs who observed the traditions of the Khalsa Panth (unshorn hair and beards for men and carrying other emblems of the militant fraternity). Many religious rituals were observed in our home. A prayer room was set apart for the Granth Sahib. One or the other member of the family had to instal it on its pedestal in the early hours of the morning and put it back to rest in a cupboard in the evening. Everyone was expected to say his morning prayer (Japji) and read a hymn or two from the scripture before he or she came to the breakfast table. The evening prayer (Rehras) was a joint affair. We took turns in reciting it while others listened. Most of us also recited the last prayer of the day (Kirtan Sohila) before switching off the lights.

My grandmother, with whom I shared a room till I was eighteen, spent the best part of the day mumbling prayers. There were frequent Akhand Paaths (non-stop reading of the Granth Sahib from cover to cover by a relay of paathees, professional priests, which takes two days and two nights). Occasionally, there was also a Sampat Paath, in which a favourite hymn had to be recited after every one of the 5,000 hymns of the Granth; this could take upwards of a fortnight. All these paaths (at which attendance was de rigueur) were accompanied by kirtans (devotional songs) sung by professional raagis (religious singers). On the birth anniversaries of the first Guru, Nanak, and the tenth Guru, Gobind Singh, as well as the martyrdom anniversaries of the fifth Guru, Arjan Dev, and the ninth Guru, Tegh Bahadur, we joined processions taken out through the streets and worshipped in public gurudwaras.

As a child of five I was initiated into reading the scriptures and could recite them by heart. At the age of seventeen, I underwent a baptismal ceremony (amrit chakna—sipping of ambrosial water), which symbolized that I had joined the Khalsa (the pure) fraternity. While in college, I began to question the value of these rituals and the need to conform to Khalsa traditions. However, I decided to go along with them rather than create trouble for myself. I took pains to understand the prayers I had been reciting. Good kirtan continued, as it does to this day, to touch my emotional chords.

Meanwhile, while studying at St. Stephens College (in Delhi), I attended Bible classes. Although the emphasis was on the New Testament and the life of Jesus Christ, it was the language of the Old Testament, particularly the Psalms, the Song of Solomon and the Book of Job, that I found myself drawn to. Later, while working on the translations of the Sikh scriptures, I found so many references in them to the Vedas, Upanishads and the epics, the Ramayana and Mahabharata (including the Bhagvad Gita, or just Gita), that I decided to study them to better comprehend the meaning of my own Gurubaani or Gurbani (the voice of the Guru). Interest in religion also made me read whatever I could on Jainism, Buddhism and later developments in Hinduism. Islam was the last religion I turned to, largely to free myself of anti-Muslim prejudices, which had been instilled in me as a child. It was during the seven years in Lahore and my close association with Manzur Qadir (a leading jurist) that I began to question many of the assumptions made by all religions. He was a Muslim but did not offer namaaz (prayer) either at home or in a mosque even on the festival of Eid; neither did his uncle, Saleem, who was India's tennis champion for many years and preferred living like a European aristocrat rather than a Muslim nawab. Being Muslim meant little to them besides an accident of birth. Neither of them bothered to make religion an issue. I did. No religion evoked much enthusiasm in my mind. By the time India gained Independence on 15 August 1947, I had gained freedom from conformist religion and openly declared myself an agnostic.

Following the publication of my two volumes on Sikh religion and history in 1963 titled *A History of the Sikhs* by Princeton University Press and the Oxford University Press, I was invited by the Spalding Foundation to deliver three lectures on Sikhism at Oxford University and also by Princeton, Swarthmore and Hawaii Universities (all three in the USA) to lecture on comparative religions. Once again I went over the scriptures and lives of the founders of the world's major religions.

## A GOOD LIFE IS THE ONLY TRUE RELIGION

Having done all this writing and lecturing, I felt mentally well equipped to express myself on religious beliefs and practices. And I feel more strongly than ever before the need to have not only a personal religion of my own but also to evolve a new set of beliefs for those Indians who have the courage to think for themselves. It is based on the assumptions that most people need some kind of faith to live with; that the emotional contents of that faith are best provided by the one into which one is born; and whose rituals have formed an integral part of his or her upbringing.

I feel what is required today is the acceptance of what is basic and rational in the religion of one's birth after removing from it the accretions of dead wood that have accumulated around it and militate against reason and common sense. I present this, the blueprint of my religion, for consideration and comment to my more enlightened countrymen.

Before I do so, I will first deal with five items which are generally regarded as the pillars of all religions: Belief in God; reverence for the founders of religions; the status of scriptures; the sanctity accorded to places of worship and pilgrimage; and the use of prayer and ritual. Since most of what I have to say on these topics may appear critical and negative, I will thereafter posit items for positive acceptance.

## The Concept of God

Every religion has its own name and concept of God. He is Jehovah, Ishwar, Parmatma, Rabb, Khuda, Allah and Waheguru. He may be symbolized in the shape of idols, animals or other natural phenomena, or He may be regarded beyond physical representation in any form. He may be believed to be the only one, a trinity or a multiplicity of Gods. However different the ways of conceiving Him, what all religions have in common are the powers they attribute to Him. He is the Creator, Preserver and Destroyer; He is Omniscient (all-knowing), Omnipotent (all-powerful) and Omnipresent; He is just, benign and merciful to the faithful and at the same time an angry God who metes out dire punishment to transgressors. Whatever He be, we have to ponder over questions posed by the philosopher-saint, Adi Shankara, over a thousand years ago and find answers to them:

> Kustwam? Ko Ham? Kutah ayatah?
> Ko mein janani? Ko mein taatah?
>
> (Who am I? Where did I come from and how?
> Who are my real father and mother who gave me birth?)

If there are none, then we have to admit that we have got the God business all wrong. Nevertheless, different religions have given different answers to these questions. These answers can be grouped into two categories: Those

## A GOOD LIFE IS THE ONLY TRUE RELIGION

given by the Judaic family of religions—Judaism, Christianity and Islam—and those given by the Hindic family of religions: Hinduism, Jainism, Buddhism and Sikhism.

The Judaic group maintains that God created the world, sent out Adam and Eve to propagate the human race and created all other forms of life. According to it, one day, all life on earth will end and there will be a Day of Judgement when people will rise from their graves to be judged for the good or evil they did in life and accordingly be sent to heaven or hell. The Judeo-Christian-Muslim view of life is linear: it has a beginning, a middle and an end.

The Hindic view of life is cyclical: There is no beginning and no end but a continuing, unending cycle of births, deaths and rebirths. There is no heaven or hell (although Hinduism has words like swarg for paradise and nark for hell) but would have you believe that reward for good deeds and punishment for evil acts are meted out in the form in which a person will be reborn. Its real equivalent to heaven is release from samsar/sansar (world) and union (yoga) with the infinite that is God. It is moksha (salvation). For the evil it will be a purgatory of rebirth in all the 84 lakh forms of life (joon) before release will be granted.

However more sophisticated the Hindic theory of samsar may appear in comparison to the simplistic Judaic version, there is as little evidence to prove its validity as there is about Adam, Eve and the Day of Judgement. The honest truth is that we do not know where we come from, whether or not there is a divine purpose in our existence on earth; nor do we know where we will go when we die. The stark truth of our ignorance is summed up in a couplet by Shad Azimabadi:

> Hikayat-e-hastee sunee
> To darmiyaan say sunee
> Na ibtida kee khabar hai,
> Na intihaa maaloom
>
> (What I have heard of the story of life
> Is only the middle
> I know not its beginning,
> I know not its end.)

Under the circumstances, the only honest answer an intelligent person can give to the question 'Is there a God?' is: 'I do not know.'

It may be recalled that Gautama Buddha was put the same question, not once but several times, by his chief disciple and cousin, Ananda. The Enlightened One did not deign to reply. The only conclusion we can draw from his silence is that he either wanted people to find out the answer themselves or it must be taken as an admission that he did not know it himself.

Maulana Abul Kalam Azad, in his scholarly commentary

on the Surah-ul Fatiha, in the first of his three-volume translation and commentary on the Quran, *Tarjuman-ul Koran*, maintains that all mankind was, at one time, monotheist but, with the eruption of different religious systems, departed from the concept of one Almighty God. He further maintains that the Islamic idea of the unity of Allah was the most advanced because it refused to give God shape or form and went beyond the Upanishadic definition in negatives—neti, neti (not this, not this)—but gave God positive attributes by calling him the Great Provider (Al-Razzaq), Ruler of the Universe (Rabb-ul Aalameen), Benevolent and Merciful (Al-Rahman, Al-Raheem) and the final arbiter of human actions (Malik-i-Yawmiddeen—Master of the Day of Reckoning).

The Maulana also quoted the Quran in support of all creation being attributed to God. His argument was much the same as that of the French Enlightenment writer-historian Francois-Marie Arouet (popularly known as Voltaire): 'We can scarcely believe that there can be a watch without a watch maker.' What neither Voltaire nor the Maulana—nor for that matter anyone else who believes that every effect must have a cause—has been able to substantiate is that if God is the cause and the world the effect, who created God in the first place? It is the primary cause, the causa causans, about which we know nothing.

Instead of entering into a pointless debate on whether

or not God exists, it is more important to bear in mind that belief in the existence of God has little bearing on making a person a good or a bad citizen. One can be a saintly person without believing in God and a detestable villain believing in Him. In my personalized religion, there is no God.

## Founders of Religions

In every religion, the founder is more revered than God. This can be ascribed to the simple reason that we know more about the founders of our faiths—be they described as prophets, messiahs, messengers, avtaars or gurus—than we know about God. They were human beings gifted with superhuman powers, which enabled them to sway the masses. With the passage of years, so many legends grew around them that they ceased to be human and became incarnations of God, His progeny, His specially chosen messengers with direct access to Him.

The classic instance of giving the messenger a higher status than God Himself is found in present-day Islam. You may make jokes about Allah, but woe betide anyone who makes the slightest insinuation against His messenger, the Prophet Mohammed: 'Ba Khudaa diwaanaa Basho, ba Mohammed hoshiaar!' (Say what you like about God, but against Mohammed, beware!) This attitude explains the fate of Salman Rushdie for having written *The Satanic*

*Verses*; the rumpus created against the eminent US economist and one-time ambassador to India, Professor John Kenneth Galbraith, when it became known that he had given his pet cat one of the names by which Prophet Mohammed was known, Ahmed; and the burning down of the offices of *The Deccan Herald* in Bangalore because it had published a short story entitled 'Mohammed the Idiot'. The story had nothing whatsoever to do with the Prophet but was about a demented man bearing the same name.

The truth of the matter is that we have hardly any reliable historical evidence on what the founders of different religions were really like. By deifying them we have done them grave injustice. We have made them incomparably good and beyond human striving. In my personalized religion, I would give prophets, avtaars and the like their due respect as important historical personages who did good to humanity. But nothing more.

## Scriptures

All scriptures are held in awe either as words of God or divinely inspired utterances. I have read them in translation many times and am astonished by the emotional fervour they arouse. The most fervent are those who never bother about the meanings of the words they chant or recite by rote. I am sure that if they bothered to read them after being translated into a language they understood, a good bit of their enthusiasm would get diluted. Without exception, their contents are unscientific—one can't blame their authors as, in their times, science was hardly advanced. In addition to being contrary to science, they are repetitive and tediously boring. Those which enshrine codes of conduct and ethics undoubtedly serve a useful purpose in providing stability to society. Some passages in most of them are also of a high literary quality. I often quote the Bible, the Quran, the Upanishads, the Gita and the Granth Sahib to buttress my arguments. But as works of literature, they do not compare with the great classics of Kalidas, Hafiz (Khwajeh Shams al-Din Muhammad Hafiz-e-Shirazi), Saadi Shirazi, William Shakespeare, Johann Wolfgang von Goethe, Leo Tolstoy, Mirza Ghalib, Rabindranath Tagore, Mohammad Iqbal, Faiz Ahmed Faiz, or even some lesser poets.

Mine is a personal reaction not shared by anyone else I have met. Most people are moved by their scriptures. They recite or chant them, swaying their heads in ecstasy as they do so, and claim to get peace of mind as a result. So who am I to tell them that their responses are conditioned by constant indoctrination and are a form of self-hypnosis? However, surely they cannot fault me when I maintain that the scriptures, for whatever they are worth, should be read and understood and not worshipped. This is what Guru Nanak had to say about people who recite prayers without understanding them:

## A GOOD LIFE IS THE ONLY TRUE RELIGION

Sudh na budh na akal sar
Akkhar ka bheyo na lahant
Nanak say nar asl khar de
je bin gun garabh karant

(They have no comprehension, no brains in their heads
Who do not bother with the meaning of words
O Nanak! Such are real donkeys
Who vaunt their pride without having done any good.)

It is ironic that it should be the followers of Nanak, who proclaimed God to be nirankar (formless) and forbade the worship of idols, who treat the compilation of his and their Gurus' writing as an idol worthy of worship. They drape the Granth Sahib in silk and brocade, rouse it in the mornings and put it to rest in the evenings, take it out in processions on holy days, and have it read by professional granthis (priests who read the Granth Sahib) all through the night while they themselves slumber. There are fixed rates for granthis: novices can be hired on cheaper terms than the adept whose pronunciation is clearer.

Sikhs are not the only ones who indulge in such gross travesty of scriptural sanctity. Hindus have their own non-stop recitations; the Muslims go one step better by distributing portions of the Quran to the congregations, which all of them read at the same time so that the entire Quran is finished in less than an hour.

## Places of Worship

I believe that the only legitimate place of worship is the home. However, there are religions like Islam, which enjoin congregational namaaz in a public mosque as a religious obligation. Christians also exhort attendance in churches on Sundays and at masses. In Hindu and Sikh temples, kirtans and kathas (sermons) are conducted regularly; without congregations to listen to them, they would lose much of their impact.

In a country like India, which has few diversions that the poor can afford, such as clubs, pubs and cinema houses, places of worship provide free, harmless entertainment in the company of like-minded people. In recent years, however, places of worship have been turned into arenas of contention and misused to propagate ideas other than those strictly religious. Some years back the most sacred site in Islam, the Kaaba, in Mecca in Saudi Arabia, was the scene of a pitched battle. In India there have been prolonged litigations over the control of mosques and temples and waqf (an endowment as per Islamic law) funds and trusts. In the early 1980s, the holiest shrine of the Sikhs, the Golden Temple in Amritsar, notably the Akal Takht, was under the control of young gun-toting men spouting hate rather than spreading the message of love that their Gurus preached. In early June 1984, Prime Minister Indira Gandhi authorized the Indian Army to

## A GOOD LIFE IS THE ONLY TRUE RELIGION

evict them, thereby deeply hurting the Sikh psyche. (This was known as Operation Bluestar.) And who can forget the demolition of the Babri Masjid at Ayodhya (in Uttar Pradesh) on 6 December 1992 by Hindu fanatics, leading to large-scale riots across the country?

I am convinced that the time has come for the government to forbid the building of any more places of worship—we have more than enough of them already—and to refuse permission to use public places for religious gatherings. And whenever a place of worship becomes a bone of contention or is misused for non-religious purposes by undesirable elements, its control and management must be taken over by the government. Places of worship have created vested interests for priests, pandas (Hindu priests well versed in genealogy), granthis, imams (those who lead the prayers in a mosque) and raagis whose livelihood depends on exploiting them. This must be put an end to. My sentiments regarding places of worship are summed up in a beautiful little couplet by Bulleh Shah, a Punjabi Sufi poet:

> Masjid ddhaa dey, Mandar ddhaa dey
> Ddhaa dey jo kuchh ddhenda.
> Ik kisey da dil na ddhavein
> Rabb dilaan vicch rehndaa
>
> (Break down the mosque, break down the temple
> Break down whatever there is besides;

But never break a human heart
That is where God Himself resides.)

## Prayer and Meditation

It can scarcely be disputed that we Indians, be we Hindus Muslims, Christians, Sikhs or Parsis, spend more time in performing religious rituals than any other people in the world. The Hindi adage, saat vaar aur aath tyohaar—there are only seven days in a week but there are eight religious festivals—is by no means an overstatement. Count the number of religious holidays, national and sectional, then add up the number of hours people spend every day in saying their prayers and visiting temples, mosques, churches and gurudwaras, the days spent in pilgrimage to holy places, the hours taken up by satsangs (religious gatherings), pravachans (religious discourses), kirtans, bhajans, jagratas (all-night singing of devotional songs), and so on. It will come to a staggering total. Then ask yourself whether a poor developing country like ours can afford to lose so many millions of man hours in pursuits that produce no material benefits? Also ask yourself whether strict adherence to a routine of prayer, ritual or telling the beads of a rosary makes a person a better human being? Is it not true that even dacoits pray for success of their nefarious missions before they embark on them? And aren't the worst tax evaders and black marketeers often devoutly religious.

## A GOOD LIFE IS THE ONLY TRUE RELIGION

On rare occasions, when I visited a gurudwara or a temple, I made it a point to watch people making obeisance before the Granth Sahib or their favourite God.

Those who took the longest time to rub their noses on the ground were usually those who more than others craved forgiveness for having lied, stolen, fornicated and made illicit money.

I concede that it is entirely up to any individual how he or she decides to spend his or her time. If they get peace of mind through prayer and performance of ritual, they have every right to pray as long as they want to and wave candelabras of incense and tinkle bells to their hearts' content. But what they, or anyone else, have no right to do is to impose their religiosity on other people. We as a people do this without consideration for the feelings and comforts of our fellow citizens. An instance of this total lack of concern for others is the use of loudspeakers calling for prayers (azaan from mosques) or blasting forth kirtans, bhajans and pravachans. The craziest examples are all-night jaagrans that disturb the sleep of entire localities. Children are unable to concentrate on their studies, the sick unable to get rest, and if there has been a death in some household, the family members are unable to mourn in silence.

Another instance of imposing one's religious practices on others is the custom of taking out processions through crowded streets which, it cannot be denied, upsets civic life. Christians and Muslims rarely take out processions. Catholics occasionally take idols of the Madonna or saints around the streets and Shia Muslims take out tazias during Moharram. But Hindus and Sikhs indulge in them as a sacred birthright. Hindu Gods and Goddesses must be periodically taken out for airing; Goddesses Kali and Durga must be taken round the streets before they are immersed in rivers; so must Ganapaty, accompanied by loud shouts of 'Ganapaty Bappa Morya'. The mammoth procession taken out annually at Jagannath Puri brings all other activity in the city to a full stop. Sikhs must take out processions on the birthdays and martyrdom anniversaries of their Gurus, no matter what Hindus or Muslims feel about them. It should be remembered that the most common cause of Hindu-Muslim riots are Hindu processions passing by mosques when Muslims are at prayer.

The government must take the lead in curbing the unnecessary exhibitions of religious fervour. It is committed through the Constitution to inculcate a scientific outlook on life. Instead of doing that, it allows official media like All India Radio and Doordarshan to propagate religions through the broadcast of celebrations and hymn singing. Religious broadcasts take up most of the time of some TV channels.

## A GOOD LIFE IS THE ONLY TRUE RELIGION

The worst part is that the juggernaut of religion rolls on, getting full media coverage. Preaching religion over official media is against the spirit of secularism; protests against it are ignored like the yapping of agnostic dogs. A long time back I saw an hour-long programme on Doordarshan on the birthday of a Nirankari guru. I have absolutely nothing against Nirankaris;* on the contrary, I have defended their right to propagate their beliefs despite hukumnamas (decrees) issued from the Akal Takht. What I found very hard to stomach were the paeans of praise showered on their young guru. There were a few sad-looking foreign young ladies constipated with virtue who read their pieces; they were followed by a succession of second-rate poets reading qaseedas (paeans) as they would sehras at a wedding. No doubt they were paid according to their skill at tukbandi (rhyming). Far from being impressed, I found the entire exercise vastly amusing and laughable. If religion is to have any meaning in present-day life, it has to be treated more seriously than chanting hallelujahs to godmen or godwomen.

All this also reminds me of my visits to Canada or the States. Whenever there, I always looked forward to Sunday mornings when many TV channels were taken over by

---

*A sect of Sikhism that holds views different from the traditional Sikhs vis-à-vis the ten Gurus.

evangelists preaching love, morality and singing praises of the Almighty. I relished those programmes for a very perverse reason: I found them hilariously comic and laughed more than I would while watching a slapstick comedy. I saw very soulful-looking men and pretty damsels dressed in virginal white turning their eyes skywards to God (who is believed to live above the clouds) and singing hosannas with full-throated fervour. The greatest 'comedians' of those god-plays used to be Reverends Jimmy Lee Swaggart and Jim Bakker. Unfortunately, both men who preached sexual morality and martial fidelity were caught pants down consorting with prostitutes.

A modern fad, which has gained widespread acceptance amongst the educated and semi-educated who wish to appear secular, is the practice of meditation. They proclaim with an air of smug superiority: 'Main mandir-vandir nahin jaata, bas meditate karta hoon. (I don't go to temples or other such places, I only meditate.)' The exercise involves sitting in the lotus pose (padmasana), regulating one's breathing and emptying the mind to prevent it from 'jumping about like a monkey' from one (thought) branch to another. This intense concentration apparently awakens the kundalini (the serpent coiled at the base of the spine), which then travels upwards through chakras (circles) till

## A GOOD LIFE IS THE ONLY TRUE RELIGION

it reaches its destination in the cranium. Then the kundalini is fully jaagrit (roused) and the person is assumed to have reached his or her goal.

What does meditation achieve? The usual answer is 'peace of mind'. If you further ask 'and what does peace of mind achieve?' you will get no answer because there is none. Peace of mind is a sterile concept, which produces nothing. The exercise may be justified as therapy for those with disturbed minds or those suffering from hypertension, but there is no evidence to prove that it enhances creativity. On the contrary, it can be established by statistical data that all the great works of art, literature, science and music were works of highly agitated minds, at times on the verge of collapse. Allama Iqbal's short prayer is pertinent:

> Khuda tujhey kisee toofan say aashna kar dey
> Key terey beher kee maujon mein iztirab natheen
>
> (May God bring a storm in your life,
> There is no agitation in the waves of your life's ocean.)

A word that constantly appears in the Allama's writings is talaatum, restlessness of the mind, as the sine qua non of creativity.

I would like to sum up all I have said about prayer, ritual and meditation in a slogan I have coined as a motto for modern India:

> Work is worship,
> but worship is not work.

My new religion for India would be primarily based on the work ethic. We have an apt motto, which needs to be put into effect: aaraam haraam hai (rest is forbidden). However, leisure time to recoup energy to resume work, which yields material benefits, ought to be provided. We must not waste time because time is precious. There is a Hadith (sayings of Prophet Mohammed) in which he is said to have exhorted (which, loosely translated, means): 'Do not waste time; time is God.' We must reject the concepts of sanyas (retirement) and vanaprastha (taking to the woods; i.e., renouncing everything) and continue to labour till we are physically able to do so. Leading idle lives on inherited or unearned incomes is as bad as being a beggar. Laws must be passed to limit the right to leave property to descendants and begging must be outlawed. Guru Nanak emphasized the work ethic in three commandments:

> Kirt karo,
> naam japo,
> vand chako
>
> (work,
> worship
> and give in charity)

Note the order of priorities. In another hymn he wrote:

## A GOOD LIFE IS THE ONLY TRUE RELIGION

Khat ghaal
kicch hatthon dey,
Nanak raah pacchaney sey

(He who earns,
and gives some of it away,
O Nanak, he has found the right way.)

He or she who does not contribute materially to society has no right to claim any benefits from it.

There are some professions, much practised in our country, which contribute nothing to society but instead do a great deal of harm to it. The most popular of them is forecasting the future through astrology, casting horoscopes, palmistry, crystal-ball-gazing and deciphering ancient texts like the Bhrigu Samhita and the Sau Saakhee. Of these, astrology is the most widespread and believed in as much by the highest placed as by the masses. Prime ministers, chief ministers, other ministers, governors, bureaucrats and businessmen regularly perform tantric rites and practise black magic, ostensibly to overcome the influence of evil stars. New ventures are undertaken only after making sure that the stars are in their proper positions.

In India, astrology has religious sanction. It must therefore be exorcised from the Indian religion of the future. That it is totally unscientific is beyond dispute. Astronomy is a science; astrology is not. What superstition is to religion, astrology is to astronomy—the illegitimate offspring of sick minds.

There are innumerable instances in our history highlighting how battles were lost because our commanders, instead of using their common sense, consulted astrologers about the most auspicious time to commence the attack. There is no evidence whatsoever to prove that marriages made after matching horoscopes do better than those consummated without consulting them. I know of the case of a leading astrologer who wrote a weekly column, 'What the Stars Foretell', for the *Hindustan Times*, who arranged his daughter's marriage after reading her and her future bridegroom's horoscopes. The marriage lasted only a few months. Belief in astrology has assumed menacing proportions and, unless banned by legal enactment, will continue to govern the lives of people to their detriment.

The ultimate purpose of religion should be to abstain from causing hurt to all living things—human beings, flora and fauna—as far as possible. Ahimsa Paramo Dharma, i.e., non-violence is the paramount religion. When it comes to humans, we have to learn to avoid hurting them. Writes Hafiz (the fourteenth-century Sufi poet):

Mai khor, mimbar ba-soz, O aatish andar Kaaba zan
Sakin-e-butkhana baash, O mardam azaari mekun

## A GOOD LIFE IS THE ONLY TRUE RELIGION

> (Drink wine, tear up the holy book, set fire to the house of God
> Go make your house in a temple full of idols;
> You may do all these, but do not hurt a man.)

Maulana Jalaluddin Rumi, a thirteenth-century Sufi poet, echoed the same sentiment:

> Dile badast aavar keh haj-e-akbar ast
> az hazaaman Kaaba, yak-e-dil behtarast
>
> (Go into your hearts, it is the greatest pilgrimage
> One heart is better than a thousand Kaabas.)

I am not sure whether we are yet in a position to outlaw the killing of animals for food because, in large parts of the world, human beings survive only by eating meat, fish and eggs. But this does not justify cruelty to animals or killing them for sport. Fortunately, in India, the hunting of animals has been banned.

Our new religion should have a vision of the future and should aim to provide measures that do not put the lives of the generations to come in jeopardy. Our population is rising at a rate suicidal to our future. If we continue to breed in the reckless way we are doing, we will continue to be short of food, clothing, housing, educational institutions and hospitals, and our cities, towns and villages will fester with slums. Family planning must be made an integral part of our religion. We must disenfranchise parents who have more than two children and forbid them from holding elective offices. We must also make sterilization of both parents on the birth of their second child compulsory. An undertaking to do so could be made a part of the vows taken at marriage. We have no right to overload an already overpopulated country.

The preservation of our environment must also become an essential part of our religion. We have the example of the Bishnoi community, which rigorously forbids the cutting of trees and killing of animals or birds. We have to go further. Felling of trees must be forbidden. The Hindu-Sikh custom of cremating the dead on funeral pyres must be stopped forthwith. There is nothing in the Hindu and Sikh religions requiring the burning of the dead with wood. Many Hindu communities in South India bury their dead. For instance, C. N. Annadurai and M. G. Ramachandran (both former chief ministers of Tamil Nadu, who died on 3 February 1969 and 24 December 1987, respectively) were buried. Jain munis (monks) too are buried. The amount of wood that is consumed in cremations is horrendous. It has been calculated that on an average more than one crore Indians die every year, of whom 80 per cent are Hindus or Sikhs. Roughly two quintals of wood is consumed in cremating one dead body, making a staggering total of millions of quintals of wood consumed every year. We are destroying our forests to dispose of our dead. The answer is not electric or gas crematoria but Hindu-Sikh cemeteries with the proviso that no tombstones are erected on graves and the land is returned to agriculture every five years. The earth is in need of rejuvenation.

Humans, when they die, should be returned to the earth from which, according to most religions, they emanate.

The use of wood for construction and furniture also needs to be severely curtailed. We have now enough synthetic substitutes to make all the buildings and furniture we need. Reafforestation and greening of our land must be given top priority. They can be easily included as a part of our religious obligations as well as become a compulsory component of our educational system. At every religious ceremony, be it the thread ceremony, baptism, marriage or death, provision should be made for planting a certain number of trees. Charities given in memory of departed souls should be devoted to the planting of forests. Students passing their school-leaving or degree exams should not be given their certificates unless they provide evidence of having planted a required number of trees and seen them grow in good health for a specified number of years.

Polluting catchment areas, rivers and lakes should be condemned as irreligious acts. The use of chemical fertilizers and pesticides, which make the land sterile and destroy bird and insect life, must also be severely curtailed.

The earth must be considered sacred, as must the lives of birds, beasts and insects. All ancient religions have something to say about the preservation of the environment as a religious duty. All we have to do is highlight these aspects and emphasize them with greater vigour.

Let me sum up my faith in a time-worn cliché: a good life is the only religion. The nineteenth-century American political leader and orator during the Golden Age of Free Thought, Robert G. Ingersoll, who was noted for his broad range of culture, put it in more felicitous language: 'Happiness is the only good; the place to be happy is here; the time to be happy is now; the way to be happy is to help others.' One of America's greatest writers, Ella Wheeler Wilcox (1850–1919), whose prolific prose and poetry are a tour de force of optimism, put the same in plainer words:

> So many gods, so many creeds, so many paths that
>     wind and wind.
> When just the art of being kind is all that the sad world
>     needs.

In fine, let me clarify my ideas of God, religion and moral values.

It is evident that all religious systems have failed us. They have generated more misunderstanding and hatred

## A GOOD LIFE IS THE ONLY TRUE RELIGION

than love and friendship. However, since some people need some sort of system of beliefs, we have to evolve a new religion that avoids the pitfalls of outworn creeds, of which we have had a bitter experience.

The process has to be dual: first wipe the slate clean and then start afresh to write a new message. What we need to demolish are the five established pillars of most religious systems: God, prophets, scriptures, prayer and places of worship.

To my way of thinking, it is not very important whether or not people believe in God, or how they visualize Him—as one, a trinity or in multiplicity; as an old, long-bearded Jehovah, in the shape of an idol, nirguna (without attributes) or sarguna (with attributes), or as an abstraction. God simply does not matter.

Founder-prophets of religions matter a great deal to people, but instead of worshipping them, they should be regarded as historical characters who brought about revolutionary changes in society.

Likewise, I would treat religious scriptures as historical writings and judge them on their literary qualities. They should not become subject matters of prayers. Places of worship should be converted to schools, colleges or hospitals, or simply preserved as historical monuments.

We must not erase the past unless we have something positive to replace it with: mental vacuum can have disastrous consequences. In my outline of a future religion man replaces God. Fellow humans should be our top priority. You don't have to worship them; only refrain from hurting them either physically or mentally.

I would place the care of all living creatures next to humans. We have no right to deprive them of life for our own sustenance. I subscribe to the Jain concept of Ahimsa Paramo Dharma and would make a strong plea for vegetarianism.

I would not include other items of food or drink amongst the don'ts. What an adult consumes of his or her own free will—be it alcohol, narcotics or tobacco is entirely his or her own business even if it does him or her harm or kills him or her.

I would also replace reciting prayers by doing good work. Instead of chanting mantras or reading scriptures, every person should set aside at least one hour of the day for social service from which he or she derives no personal benefit but is beneficial for his or her fellow beings or animals. It should be nishkama seva (selfless service); teaching children, tending the sick or the handicapped, cleaning drains. Or whatever.

And finally, before retiring for the night, everyone should spend at least fifteen minutes entirely with himself or herself to review what he or she has done that day. I would suggest instead of meditating you should look at

## A GOOD LIFE IS THE ONLY TRUE RELIGION

your own image in a mirror, look squarely into the reflection of your own eyes and ask yourself: 'Did I hurt anyone today? If so, I must make amends tomorrow. Did I do anything to lighten another's burden, sorrow or pain today? If not I must double my efforts tomorrow.' It is not very easy to face one's own conscience, but it is the ultimate test which one must pass. For me this test was beautifully worded by William Shakespeare in *Hamlet*.

> This above all: To thine own self be true,
> And it must follow as the night the day,
> Thou canst not then be false to any man.

I suggest that on religious festivals, after performing expected rituals like going to temples, mosques, churches or gurudwaras, people should spend a little time—no more than half an hour—alone in silence and ask themselves: 'What does my religion really means to me?' Hindus could do this on Ram Navami or Diwali, Muslims on Eid-ul-Fitr, Christians on Christmas, Sikhs on the birth anniversary of the founder of Sikhism—Guru Nanak.

On Guru Nanak's birth anniversary (21 November 2010) I tried to answer the question: How much of a Sikh am I? And drew up a list of answers. Although I do not practise my religious rituals, I have a sense of belonging to the Sikh community. Whatever happens to it is of concern to me and I speak up or write about it.

## ON RELIGION

I think that speculating about where we come from and where we go after we die is a waste of time. No one has the foggiest idea. What we should be concerned about is what we do in our lives on earth. I have imbibed what I think are the basics of Sikhism as I see it now. I regard truth to be the essence of religion and a must for life.

I do my best not to lie because lying requires cunning to cover up the lies you have told before. Truth does not require brains.

As mentioned earlier, earn your own living and share some of it with others, said Guru Nanak.

I try not to hurt others' feelings. If I have done so, I try to cleanse my conscience by tendering an apology before the year is out.

I have also imbibed the motto: 'Chardi Kalan—ever remain in buoyant spirits, never say die'. Ponder over it. Try it out.

# THE POWER OF PRAYER AND MIRACLES

All religions have a few words believed to have powerful protective and curative potential. It is difficult to unravel the mystery behind them. In Hinduism we have the mystic syllable Om or Aum. It is chanted in its elongated form and believed to have the entire range of sounds in it. Intoned by itself or in combination with one of the names of God, Hari, as Hari Om, it does produce a soothing effect on jangled nerves and brings peace to the mind. The Sikh equivalent Ek Onkar (there is one God) is derived from it, but does not enjoy the same popularity among Sikhs as does Om among Hindus.

The Muslims do not have any single word to match Om, but they do have some which, like Allah-o-Akbar, are repeated while telling the beads of a rosary. They also recite select passages of the Quran which are believed to be more powerful than others. The most frequently quoted is, of course, the opening lines of the holy book, *Al-Fatihah*:

> All praise be to Allah
> Lord of all the worlds,
> Most beneficent, ever merciful,
> King of the Day of Judgement,
> You alone we worship, and to You alone we turn for
>     help.
> Guide us (O Lord) to the path that is straight,
> The path of those You have blessed,
> Not of those who have earned Your anger, nor those
>     who have gone astray.
>
> —Ahmed Ali

Next to the *Fatihah*, the second most popular verse is the 'Ayat-ul-Qursi', the throne verse:

> God: There is no God but He, the living, sustaining,
>     ever self-subsisting.
> Neither does somnolence affect Him nor sleep.
> To Him belongs all that is in the heavens and the earth;
> And who can intercede with Him except by His leave?
> Known to Him is all that is present before men and
>     what is hidden
> (in time past and time future) and to even a little of His
>     knowledge can they grasp except what He will.

## THE POWER OF PRAYER AND MIRACLES

> His set extends over heavens and the earth and
> He tires not protecting them:
> He alone is all high and supreme.
> There is no compulsion in matter of faith.
> Distinct is the way of guidance now from error.
> He who turns away from the forces of evil
> And believes in God, will surely hold fast
> To a handle that is strong and unbreakable,
> For God hears all and knows everything.
> 
> —Ahmed Ali

The 'Ayat-ul-Qursi' is embossed on medallions and worn by Muslim ladies attached to their necklaces. It is also the most popularly quoted verse on Muslim graves. The third in popularity are lines from Surah Yaseen. This Surah is also a favourite citation on mausoleums. On the entrance gate of the Taj Mahal, it is reproduced in full.

Among Hindus, the mantra regarded as the most powerful is the Gayatri from the Yajur Veda. To me it appeared as an invocation to the sun and I could not decipher any hidden meaning in it. I turned to my one-time Hindi teacher (I studied Hindi only for two years before I turned to Urdu) for an explanation. Dr Dashrath Ojha, who retired as a professor of Hindi and Sanskrit of Delhi University some years ago, was kind enough to illumine my mind. I share his explanation. First the mantra:

Om bhur bhuvah swah
Tat savitur varenyam
Bhargo devasya dhimahi
Dhiyo yo nah prachodayat.

Let us meditate on God, His glorious attributes, who is the basis of everything in this universe as its creator, who is fit to be worshipped as a omnipresent, omnipotent, omniscient and self-existent conscious being, who removes all ignorance and impurities from the mind and purifies and sharpens our intellect... May God enlighten our intellects.

Dr Ojha advises that in order to comprehend the full meaning of the mantra, the reciter must pause at the end of each line and let the meaning sink in.

After the incantation Om is 'Bhur bhuva swah', meaning on earth (bhur), in the sky (bhuva) and in the heavens above the sun (swah). 'Tat' stands for God, 'savitur' God as the Creator and the power that sustains creation; 'Varenyam' indicates that God is transcendent; 'bhargo' that He is the light that dispels darkness and purifies impurities; 'devasya'—He is the light behind all lights and the bestower of happiness; 'dhimahi' is the exhortation to meditate on Him; 'dhiyo yo' stands for intellect; 'nah' for ours and 'prachodayat' is the prayer that God may direct our energies towards good deeds, thoughts and conduct.

According to Dr Ojha, the purpose of reciting the

Gayatri Mantra is as follows: 'As this mantra invokes an integrated form of endless and beginningless God, all limitations which are normally found in the worship of a personal god or goddess are totally absent in its goal. As such it helps to clean our mind of its impurities in totality as and when it expands in tune with the meaning of its repetition. Thus, gradually, this mantra helps us to possess an enlightened intellect. This enables us to know more and more about God in meditation and the mysteries of nature through intellect when it is directed towards objects. This also makes us maintain constant awareness of the very basis of our existence. As this mantra directs the imagination of the mind to a limitless state, it strikes at the very root of our basic desires and instincts, not necessarily of this present life, but also many past lives.'

There is something inherent in all religious systems which makes them intolerant towards others. This phenomenon is particularly noticeable when a section of believers break away from the main body to recognize sub-prophets of their own with their separate scriptures, places of worship and social organizations. No religious system is known to have escaped the cancer of intolerance.

Hinduism, which makes lofty claims of being the most tolerant of religions (the caste system notwithstanding) was unable to contain itself either against Jainism or Buddhism, which broke away from it. When Hinduism came back into its own, it wreaked terrible vengeance against Jains and Buddhists and virtually wiped them out as separate communities.

Judaism was unable to accept the emergence of Christ and denounced Him as a heretic. Christians never forgave the Jews for what they did to their Messiah and continue to persecute them to this day. Then Christianity splintered into many churches—Catholic, Greek Orthodox, Protestant and dozens of others. Catholics and Protestants have waged wars against each other and perpetrated massacres of each others' populations. When Islam rose out of paganism, Judaism and Christianity, Muslims suffered the same fate. They repaid the Jews and the Christians in the same way.

Smaller religious communities like the Sikhs did not escape this malaise either. While they were able to make adjustments with the numerically more powerful Hindus and Muslims, they could not tolerate sub-communities which broke away from the Sikh mainstream.

Two groups, the Namdharis and the Nirankaris, which recognized gurus of their own, were ostracized. Neither of them is allowed inside gurdwaras and no amritdhari may have matrimonial relationship with them. Bhindranwale turned the wiping out of Nirankaris into an article of faith. Their sacred books, *Avtar Bani* and *Yugpurush*, were condemned as derogatory of the Sikh gurus (I was unable

## THE POWER OF PRAYER AND MIRACLES

to locate anything offensive in them), and Baba Gurbachan Singh was murdered.

From the outside, Islam gives the impression of being a unified, monolithic religious group. It is nothing of the sort. It broke into two immediately after the death of Prophet Muhammad. The larger section accepted the succession of the first three Caliphs—Abu Bakr, Omar and Othman. A smaller group regarded them as usurpers and recognized only Ali, the Prophet's son-in-law, as the true successor. Ever since, the Islamic world has been split into the Shias and Sunnis. Their hostility continues to this day. While the Sunnis have not had many breakaway groups and only follow different schools of jurisprudence, the Shias have virtually dozens of sub-groups with their own mosques, rituals and graveyards.

Muslim intolerance towards breakaway groups—the Bahais and the Quadianis—has been noticeably fierce. Hundreds of Bahais were executed in Iran for no crime except being Bahais during the reign of Ayatollah Khomeini. Pakistanis did not lag behind in their fervour in persecuting Quadianis. This group, which branched out in 1889 under the leadership of Mirza Ghulam Ahmed of Quadian (now in Indian Punjab) has done more to spread the message of Islam in Africa and Europe than any other set of Muslim missionaries. It has also produced some very distinguished men like Chaudhary Zaffarullah Khan, judge of the Supreme Court and later foreign minister of Pakistan, and Professor Abdus Salam, the only Pakistani winner of the Nobel Prize. But they have, nevertheless, been the target of Muslim fundamentalism. Their township, Rabwah, along the Jhelum, witnessed a lot of violence before the country's highest judiciary declared Ahmediyas to be non-Muslims. They are not allowed to call for prayer from the minarets of their mosques and not even allowed to describe themselves as Muslims. They have declared themselves a minority.

The only point of contention is that the ulema maintains that Islam recognizes Muhammad as the last of the Prophets (Khatmun Nabi) and anyone who accepts a successor is a heretic. The Ahmediyas strenuously deny that they ever question Muhammad's singular Prophethood and look upon their Mirza Sahib and his successors simply as guides. This is not good enough for the Pakistani ulema.

The fact that the Aga Khan is regarded as a living God by his Ismaili followers and that there are innumerable Muslim sects based on the worship of pirs is considered besides the point. Logic has never been the strong point of any established religion. Nor has there been room for the accommodation of a different point of view in the minds of religious bigots.

## THE POWER OF PRAYER AND MIRACLES

Mrs Indira Gandhi ordered the Indian Army into the Golden Temple. Her Sikh bodyguards avenged the insult by killing her. Sikhs killed Mrs Gandhi, so Hindus avenged her murder by killing thousands of Sikhs. Mrs Gandhi's murderers were hanged so Khalistani terrorists took revenge by hanging a few innocent Hindus. The spirit of revenge is deeply ingrained in the human psyche. It is not an animal instinct because animals do not kill to take revenge, only in self-defence or for food.

All religious systems have tried in their own ways to exorcise the spirit of revenge from the human mind. Some have achieved notable successes in this direction by adopting penal codes which forbid people settling their scores themselves and making punishment for crime the business of the state.

This significant step was taken in the transition from the Old to the New Testament. Judaism sanctioned 'an eye for an eye, a tooth for a tooth'. In the Sermon on the Mount, which forms the most important part of the New Testament, Jesus is quoted as preaching: 'Ye have heard that it hath been said, an eye for an eye, a tooth for a tooth. But I say unto you, that ye resist not evil; but whosoever shall smite thee on the right cheek, turn to him the other also. And if any man shall sue thee at the law, and take away the coat, let him have the cloak also' (Matthew 5:39-40).

One must be fair to Judaism. Although it sanctioned retaliation in equal measure, it did not justify a person taking the law into his own hands. It was not for the individual whose eye had been pierced or tooth knocked out to execute revenge but to lodge a complaint and submit to a court's judgement whether or not the man who did him harm was to be punished in the same manner or compensated by a sum of money. 'Love thy neighbour as thyself' was also an integral part of the Judaic faith.

Islam, which took a great deal from Judaism and Christianity, made a similar compromise between crime and punishment. It accepted the principle of an eye for an eye, but allowed compensation in place of similar punishment as legitimate and elevated forgiveness to the pedestal of supreme virtue.

Badla or revenge has never been sanctioned by any of the religious systems of Hinduism, Jainism, Buddhism or Sikhism. Jainism made Ahimsa Paramo Dharma—the supreme religion—and even forbade the killing of animals for food. Likewise, the Buddha preached non-violence in the face of violence. Sikhism of the first nine Gurus as compiled in the Granth Sahib also preaches the moral superiority of turning the other cheek over retaliation. Among the most-quoted lines is from the Muslim divine Baba Fareed:

Jo tain maara mukkian
Tina na maaren ghum
Apanery ghar jai ke
Payr tina de choom

(Those who hit you with their fists
Do not turn and hit them back;
Seek them out in their homes
And kiss their feet.)

Guru Gobind Singh, the last of the Gurus, turned the Sikhs into a militant fraternity and exhorted dharmayuddha—the battle of righteousness—in the face of unwarranted aggression. But he did not justify a person taking the law into his own hands. And sanctioned the use of force by a people only after all other means had been tried and had failed-it was only then that they were to draw the sword. In a memorable passage he wrote: 'I came into the world charged with the duty to uphold the right in every place, to destroy sin and evil. Holy men, know it well in your hearts that the only reason I took birth was to see that righteousness may flourish: that the good may live and tyrants be torn out by their roots.'

There are other aspects of the spirit of the revenge that need to be considered. There may be some justification for wanting to avenge the wrong done to you by paying the wrongdoer in the same coin. To wit:

## ON RELIGION

Tit for Tat;
Remember that;
You killed my dog,
I'll kill your cat.

You may not rest in peace till you have maimed or murdered the man who raped your child. Such levelling of scores has its own logic. But when vengeance is sought to be extended to people of the wrongdoer's caste or community, its implications can be horrifying. This unfortunately has become a regular pattern of our lives. When one man desecrates a place of worship we not only desecrate his people's place of worship, but also seek to avenge ourselves against his clan or community. The sickening incidents of communal riots bear testimony to this extended spirit of revenge. And often we extend the domain of vengeance against the entire society by organizing bandhs and gheraos, derailing trains, burning buses and causing damage to public property.

It would be naïve to expect that religious sermons will curb the desire to seek revenge. Forgiveness is a very rare commodity. There are not many in the world who, like Jesus Christ on the cross, would say of his tormentors: 'Lord, forgive them for they know not what they do.' However hard it may be to forgive the wrongdoer, it is the only antidote to badla.

## THE POWER OF PRAYER AND MIRACLES

Israel Zangwill has a lovely short story about how a place can acquire sanctity and people who have blind faith at times benefit from it. It is about a remote village in eastern Poland where lived a poor Jewish woodcutter with his young wife. Near their home lived a middle-aged woman with her son who had been born paralytic. She had spent whatever she had to have him treated, but it had been of no avail.

Come Christmas and the village and the surrounding country was under a layer of snow. The woodcutter had made a little money selling firewood and was looking forward to eating a square meal after a long while. Early on the morning of Christmas Day, the woodcutter's wife went out into the woods to pick holly and mistletoe to decorate her home.

After she had gathered what she wanted, she came by a pond frozen with ice. It occurred to her that she had not had a bath for many days and her husband, though Jewish, might wish to celebrate the occasion in other ways. She took off her clothes, smashed the ice and jumped into the icy water. No sooner had she done so than she heard human voices approaching. She got out of the pool, gathered her clothes and ran naked into the woods towards her home.

The human voices belonged to two farmers who happened to be out with their guns to see if they could get a wild hare or some other game for their Christmas dinner. They saw the figure of a young girl come out of the icy pool and disappear in the snows. They came back to the village and spread the story that they had seen the Virgin Mary. Soon the entire village was out to see the pond. All the signs of someone having bathed in it were there. Surely, if the Virgin had come there, the water must be blest.

The middle-aged widow heard the story. She picked up her paralysed son in her arms and hurried to the pond. With full faith that a miracle would happen, she ducked her son in the chilly water. The shock did to the boy what medicines and therapy had failed to do. He was cured of his paralysis.

The story of the miracle cure spread like wildfire. The trickle of pilgrims became a regular stream. The Jewish woodcutter and his wife made good business. They filled small phials with water from the pond and sold it at high prices for its medicinal properties. The site was examined by a representative of the Pope who confirmed that the Holy Virgin had indeed visited the place and many people had been cured of their ailments by drinking the water. A huge cathedral was built in the village and it soon became a place of pilgrimage. The one to benefit the most was the poor Jewish woodcutter who, through the sale of his land and millions of bottles full of 'sacred' water, became a millionaire.

## THE POWER OF PRAYER AND MIRACLES

Zangwill's story is, of course, apocryphal. But it does contain an element of truth in so far as people who have blind faith in miracles are known to have miraculous recoveries. I am not sure of the origin of Lourdes in France, but eveyone who goes there will see innumerable crutches abandoned by those who could not walk as evidence of their having been healed. Millions go to Lourdes for treatment. Perhaps a handful, already on the verge of being healed, get healed. But they perpetuate the legend that such miracles are possible.

Belief in miracles exists in every religious system. The outstanding example is the Hindus' belief in the purifying qualities of the waters of the Ganga and various 'sacred' tanks such as those at Kurukshetra and Pushkar near Ajmer. The 'holy dip' is a uniquely Hindu-Sikh phenomenon. Stellar constellations determine the more auspicious days like the Kumbhs when the ritual bath is said to be more beneficial. Some even wipe out all sins committed in the past.

Guru Nanak proclaimed: 'I have no miracle save the name of the Lord.' Despite that, many miracles have become attached to his name and the places he visited. A freshwater spring, not far from Rawalpindi, has an overhanging rock with the imprint of a human palm dug into it. The faithful believe it is the palm of Guru Nanak as he stretched out his hand to stop a boulder loosened by an envious Muslim pir on him. The gurdwara that has come up on the site is known as Panja Sahib. There is an annual pilgrimage of Sikhs from all over the world to this gurdwara.

There is another place in the hills where there is a tree growing reetha, which is normally very bitter. The fruit of this particular tree is very sweet because the Guru sat under its shade. It is no use telling devout Sikhs that there is in fact a botanical species of reetha which bears sweet fruit.

As with the Hindus, so with the Sikhs, waters of temple tanks are endowed with sanctity. Bathing in 'the pool of nectar' from which Amritsar derives its name is de rigeur for all pilgrims. In addition, water from a sacred spot such as Har ki Pauri in Haridwar as well as behind the central shrine of the Golden Temple is drunk with reverence and collected in bottles to take home for relatives. The same reverence is accorded to the spring water of Gurdwara Bangla Sahib in New Delhi. Here the infant Guru Harikishen lived for a while before he succumbed to smallpox.

It can hardly be maintained that belief in miracles is an integral part of religion. Many devoutly religious people scoff at them as spurious accretions to beguile the superstitious and the stupid. Indeed, a case could be made out to ban propagation of miracles for the harm they do to gullible people. Many years ago there was a film made called *Nanak Naam Jahaz Hai* (the name of Nanak is a ship, to take you across the waters of life). The theme was of a young man who lost his sight in an accident. When all medical treatment failed, he undertook a pilgrimage to the major gurdwaras. Ultimately, at the Harmandir in Amritsar, a divine light came out of the temple and restored his vision. Millions of Sikhs and Hindus saw this film many times. The film producer made his millions. And spread a message of crass superstition.

Miracles are the biggest money-spinners of institutionalized religion.

# BEING AN AGNOSTIC

I once wrote an article on why I am an agnostic for the Weekly of the Malayala Manorama group of papers. I got much greater response than expected: we Indians have a consuming interest in matters of the spirit. Understandably, most of the letters refuted my contention that since we know nothing about God, belief or disbelief in his existence has little or no bearing on a person's character. We should not waste time in prayer or worship. Of the innumerable letters, one written by N. Mahadevan living in retirement in a Senior Citizens' Home near Kovalam impressed me with its lucidity and approach to the problem. He wrote: 'In the year 1938, one evening, I was going up a hill near Matunga in Bombay, sunk in thought, quite oblivious of the surroundings, with rain pouring on my head. There was a purple flower in a plant in a cleft in a rock; the eye registered it but the brain didn't, being otherwise engaged. I sat on a rock and looked back at the flower.

'Why, I pondered, does a plant have a flower? The flower is the sexual part of the plant. Like some animals, flowers exude a powerful and seductive odour when ready for mating. This attracts a multitude of bees, birds and butterflies to join in a Saturnalian rite of fecundation. In case the odour fails to attract, the flower also has a different colour and produces honey. That is, it tries every device to get itself fertilized. What beautiful patterns and variegated hues in the flowers! Flowers that remain unfertilized continue to emit a strong fragrance for as long as eight days: whereas once impregnated, the flower ceases to exude its fragrance.

'After fertilization, the flower ceases to exist. It drops off and in its place appears the green stage of the fruit. When the seed which contains the immortality of the plant is ready for propagation, the fruit which contains it undergoes a remarkable change. It changes colour, it emits a scent, and it has an inviting taste so that any of these qualities may attract a bird or beast to come to the fruit, pick it and eat it. The seed is enclosed in a hard shell and is often unpleasant to taste, so the eater of the fruit drops it. Down comes the rain, and from the seed comes a replica of the plant. The huge banyan tree is contained in a seed which can be packed thousands to an ounce. The blueprint is there in the tiny seed. And, given the right conditions, the banyan has reproduced itself.

'Am I to understand that a plant that has neither brain nor a nervous system thought up or evolved this intricate system of propagating itself? No. Even a Nobel Prize-winning scientist cannot produce a leaf or a blade of grass in his laboratory. It is not the plant as we see it that is producing this marvel. A power beyond our comprehension is manifesting itself through the plant, through the bee that pollinates its flower, through the bird that eats the fruit and disperses the seed and as I the observer, who is overwhelmed at the sudden unexpected insight into the mystery of life.'

Agnostics will go along with Mahadevan upto this point. But no further. When he takes what he calls 'the quantum leap beyond rationality', we prefer to stay back on firmer ground. Why should a thinking human being abandon the one thing that differentiates him from the animal world—his faculty of reasoning? Mahadevan quotes St. Augustine:

> My mind in a swift flash of perception attained the Absolute Being, the Ultimate and One Reality. All that is. Then verily I saw and understood. I could not sustain the sight of Infinity and Eternal Reality. It was a glimpse, transcient, a second's space.

I agree with Mahadevan that reason and logic have their limitations and are unable to probe into the ultimate mystery of our existence. The Taittiriya Upanishad affirms that it is beyond the reach of speech and thought: Yato vacho nivartante: sprapya manasa saha. (From where speech returns: even the mind (thoughts) without reaching it.

We end up being where we were. Believers would have us fly across to God on the magic carpet of faith. We agnostics would like a solid, concrete bridge of reason to cross over from the known to the unknown. Till then, their religion for them, our doubts to us.

# A JUST GOD?

A four-year-old boy, the only child of his parents, was on his way back from school. As is usual with children on their return journey, he was impatient to get back home. Without bothering to look on either side, he ran across the road and was knocked down by a speeding truck and killed instantaneously. The truck driver sped away and was never traced. An innocent life was lost, the man who took his life escaped punishment. Is there a God? An all-powerful and just God? The Holy Book promises: No ills befall the righteous, but the wicked are filled with trouble (Proverbs). The Holy Book asks: Consider, what innocent ever perished, or where have the righteous been destroyed? (Job). Let those who believe in God and in His infinite merely explain why a child whose parents had committed no sin had pain inflicted on them and then the man who

## A JUST GOD?

caused them suffering went scot free. I will not buy the theory that we pay for sins committed in a previous life or will be compensated in the life hereafter. There is no evidence whatsoever of Samskara, it is no more than what Ghalib described:

> Dil bahlaaney ko khayaal achha hai
>
> (It is a good idea to befool the mind)

I go along with Job in believing that God (if there is one) is above notions of fairness and moral rules, that apply to us mortals. However, men of faith never tire of preaching that you should look within yourself and you will find all the answers to your questions.

The book of Job ends with Job's wife praying:

> The candles in churches are out. The stars have gone out in the sky. Blow on the coal of the heart and we'll see by and by.

Strange coincidence, almost exactly the same is expressed in an Urdu couplet in almost the same words:

> Bujh rahey hain chiraagh dair-o-haram
> Dil jalao ke roshni kam hai

I have burnt my heart thinking about the existence of God. And the more I think the more I am convinced that He is an illusion. And even if there be an all-powerful creator and a destroyer, He is not a just Preserver according to the norms of justice as I understand them.

# THE QUESTION OF MORALITY

There is a trading community of north-western India and the adjoining areas of Pakistan that is as renowned for its scrupulous observance of religious rituals as it is for its unscrupulous methods of business. To this community are ascribed the following lines in Potthohaaree (or Pothwari) dialect, spoken in and around the districts of Rawalpindi and Campbellpur:

>Koor vee aseen mareney aan,
>Ghat vee aseen toleyney aan,
>Par sacchey patshah
>Aseen naan vee teyra lainey aan

>(Lies we often tell,
>Short we do often measure,
>But true Lord,
>Your name we also take.)

These lines pithily sum up the divorce between the practice of religion and the precepts of morality that bedevils the Indian society today. It would be instructive to know why and when this divorce took place, and whether there is any possibility of bringing the two together again. In order to do so we need to examine the origins of religion and its subsequent development.

First, the genesis of religion lies in the fear of the unknown. While fear continues to be the main reason for the hold of religion over the ignorant masses, the desire to know the truth about the unknown remains the chief preoccupation of religious philosophers who want to know how life began, its purpose and the possibility of its continuance after death. All this came to be summed up in the concept of God as the trinity of the Creator, Preserver and Destroyer. It was at a later stage of civilization that religion extended its sphere of activity to include making laws for society. This came about when it was discovered that the fear of the unknown God was a more effective means of preventing men from hurting each other, from stealing each others properties, slaves or wives than the scaffold or the lash.

Secondly, having established a precedent, religion further extended its sphere by making rules of social intercourse. For example: who could marry and who could not; the number of wives a man could have; and even prescribing rules of diet and hygiene as if they were divinely ordained. In this period of development came the laws of Solomon, Moses's Ten Commandments, the Code of Man, the concept of halal (just) and haram (unlawful/forbidden) enunciated in the Holy Koran and the tradition of the Prophet (Hadith). Later religions like Sikhism likewise evolved their own sets of dos and don'ts, which were spelt out in their Rahatnamas. So, a whole lot of traditions were built up by different religious groups: Catholics could not eat meat on Fridays; Hindus were forbidden from eating beef; Jains could not consume flesh of any kind or any vegetable grown under the earth; Jews and Muslims could eat no pork; Sikhs could not eat non-jhatka meat or take tobacco in any form. None of these rules could be regarded strictly as within the purview of religion, but since religion provided self-imposed restrictions, in due course, they assumed dominant roles in their respective religious groups.

The third development vis-a-vis religion was introspective: a looking within oneself to examine one's own behaviour to make a personal balance sheet of one's own conduct. Had one been unfair in dealing with others or succumbed to some temptation? This usually took the form of meditation, prayer, telling the beads of the rosary, and other similar practices designed to make one better as well as restore peace of mind.

When a new religious system came into existence, the three functions were performed by the founder. After his death they required the services of three different people: the speculative by the philosopher; law enforcement by the priest—qadi or mullah; and the introspective by the guide—guru or peer. As society advanced from the medieval to modern times, the state gradually deprived these functionaries of their religious duties. The role of religion in human conduct began to be diminished. At the same time, since religious theories about the origin of the universe and after-life failed to convince an increasingly sceptical generation and scientists admitted their limitations in probing these mysteries, soothsayers, armed with their paraphernalia, including sky charts, palm impressions, playing cards and even tea leaves and coffee cups (which they claimed helped them look into the past and future), came into their own; the astrologer took over from the astronomer and the palmist from the futurologist. These charlatans gained widespread acceptance by passing themselves off as men and women of religion. As in the world of commerce, so in the world of religion, bad currency drove out the good.

Depriving religion of its law-making and law-enforcing functions was carried out with greater thoroughness and with more serious consequences with the passage of time. The state became the law maker, the law administrator

## THE QUESTION OF MORALITY

and the final arbiter. Civil and criminal codes replaced religious codes, leaving out of their purview pointless prescriptions about diet, ritual and external forms, which became the principal preoccupations of organized religions. Thus, religious censorship in the form of ostracism came to be confined to trivia: If you ate flesh, garlic, onions and so on, you would be regarded by Jainis as a non-Jain; if you ate beef, you could become a Hindu outcaste; eating pork (by the Jews or Muslims) brought on your head the wrath of the rabbi and the mullah; and clipping hair and smoking (by a Sikh) could lead to denunciation by the Khalsa Panth. But when it came to aspects that mattered, like murder, rape, arson, robbery, stealing or seducing another's wife, it was no longer the fear or religious censure that was the ultimate deterrent but the hangman's rope, solitary confinement in a prison cell and a policeman's baton. This was a great pity because the self-restraint that religion had inculcated was gone, and when administration of law and order fell into desuetude (as in India in recent years) criminal instincts, which religious persuasion had kept under control, began to resurface.

People committed crimes because their consciences were undisturbed; they learnt to square their lying and cheating by paying lip service to God, by displaying external symbolism and performing rituals. Moral values went completely haywire. Lying, which was condemned as a sin by religion but not punished by secular law (unless on oath in court), became common. Deviations from what were regarded as normal pattern of behaviour in matters of sex assumed exaggerated importance. While in the advanced societies of the West, adultery and homosexuality came to be regarded as people's private business, with us Indians they became matters of public censure. A 'godless' West liberated itself of sexual inhibitions but learnt to be more truthful; a 'religious' India learnt to forgive liars and cheaters but condemned lechers and sodomists. The cleanest bill of moral health that could be paid to an Indian by Indians was his being naadey da succha—having the purity of the pyjama cord. Paradoxically, with the loosening of the hold of religion, we also lost our respect for women as mothers, sisters and daughters and incidents of 'eve teasing' and rape increased.

There remains another aspect of religion: an individual's personal equation with himself or herself. If he or she was unhappy, or if his or her mind was disturbed, he or she sought guidance from his or her guru and, according to the latter's instructions, chanted appropriate mantras, did yoga asanas and meditation to bring peace to his or her tortured mind. In the West, these functions came to be largely performed by the psychiatrists, although some godmen and godwomen flourished.

## THE QUESTION OF MORALITY

It will be evident from the foregoing discussion that the role of religion in present-day Indian society has shrunk to minimal proportions. Instead of bringing the best out of human beings, religion now brings out the worst in us by providing facile means of forgiveness through performance of pilgrimage or some trite form of penance or the intercession of godmen. We have to either give a totally modern reorientation to religion or scrap it altogether.

A country as vast and as populous as India, and with such a high proportion of illiterate and deprived people, can never abolish religion; nor can it afford religion being perverted. There is enough tolerance of spirit among Indians of all religions to accept each other's concept of God and allow each other to individually pursue the quest for peace of mind. What has faded into the background and needs to be restored to its legitimate primacy is religion as a social phenomenon setting out rules how people should conduct themselves towards their fellow human beings. This I suggest can be done by re-elevating Truth in all its dimensions to the status of God: as an abstract concept as another word for God; as the principle of behaviour towards one's fellow beings; and as the touchstone of one's conscience. It is only when this many-splendoured Truth becomes the object of our worship, our code of conduct and the healing balm for our souls, that religion and morality will become reunited as two sides of the same golden coin.

# GOD ON SALE

There was a time when I used to look forward to Thursday afternoons and to spending a couple of hours at the mausoleum of Hazrat Nizamuddin Auliya (123&-1325) in New Delhi. Although beggars lined the long corridors leading to the graves of the Peer Sahib and the renowned musician, scholar and poet, Amir Khusrau, once you got past them you were left in peace to enjoy the qawwalis sung in the courtyard.

Soon, the mujawwars (caretakers) of the shrine got to know of me. Every time I went there, someone or the other approached me with a receipt book and a ballpoint pen in hand. Would I make a donation for the langar (free kitchen) and upkeep of the place? After a while I stopped going to Nizamuddin.

There was a time when I used to look forward to going

to Haridwar for Purnima (full moon). The worship of the river Ganga at sunset at Har Ki Pauri with lit candelabras and leaf boats with flickering oil lamps floating down the river presented a truly magical sight. Seeing the Ganga in moonlight was a mystic experience.

I was younger and could brush aside persistent beggars, pandas (priests who keep genealogical records), purohits (priests) and the innumerably innumerable so-called charitable organizations who surrounded me with the standard receipt books and ballpoint pens soliciting contributions for gowshalas (cow sheds), ashrams and other institutions. I stopped going to Haridwar.

It was the same at Varanasi. The one and the only time I went to Puri (in Orissa) to see the Jagannath temple, I was unable to step out of the car because hordes of pandas were clamouring for my attention and claiming to be my family purohits.

I have never been much of a gurudwara-goer. But on the rare occasions I visited gurudwaras, I never placed any money in front of the Granth Sahib or in the golak (donation box). I have enough evidence of money being misappropriated by members of caretaker committees, granthis and sewadars (volunteers who offer their services to the gurudwaras). Whatever daswandh (one-tenth) of my earnings I wished to give for charity, I gave to Bhagat

Puran Singh (a well-known philanthropist), Mother Teresa or directly to people engaged in good works.

The commercialization of religious rituals was exposed, in all its crass vulgarity, decades ago, by the trouble that brewed in the temples of Badrinath and Kedarnath (high in the Himalayas in Uttarakhand). These temples are manned by Namboodri Brahmins from Kerala. None but they could enter the sanctum sanctorum or touch the deities enshrined within.

Apart from drawing regular monthly salaries, they had established a claim to seven-and-a-half per cent of the offering made at the temples. Besides the Namboodris holding the rank of high priests (rawals), there are pandits and Vedpathaks (those familiar with the Vedas) with different functions allotted to them. Rituals are rated like menus of an expensive restaurant. The entire priestly fraternity of Badrinath and Kedarnath were up in arms because the commissions of its members from the offerings were sought to be reduced; they threatened to stop performing rituals, bathe the deities or offer prayers on behalf of pilgrims.

And the less said about the high-profile ashrams which have mushroomed across the length and breadth of the country, under the patronage of jet-setting babas, gurus, and matajis, the better. Look at the cash, solid gold and silver amounting to crores and crores recovered from the ashram of Satya Sai Baba at Puttaparthi in Andhra Pradesh! Who could have imagined the twenty-four-year-old Karmapa with crores in cash and that too in various foreign currencies of the world stacked away in his temple-residence in Sidhbari in Dharamsala (Himachal Pradesh)? Look at the huge empires created by the likes of the yoga guru Ramdev and some others, who have fallen afoul of the law. For instance, the spiritual guru, Asaram Bapu, with his headquarters at Ahmedabad in Gujarat and with many ashrams under his wing, had been accused of several crimes, including murder, land encroachment and tax evasion. However, the charges could not be proved. Another guru (with a huge following), accused of murder and also sexual misconduct, was Gurmeet Rahim, who heads an organization known as Dera Sacha Sauda, based in Sirsa, Haryana. Yet another guru, Swami Nithyananda (with his base at Bangalore) was involved in a sex scandal and caught on camera. He has claimed that the images in the video—telecast by a South Indian news channel and also available on the Internet—have been morphed. It seems that now our so-called religious and spiritual gurus too are in direct competition with our corrupt political netas.

Priests, raagis and other similar figures have acquired

vested interests in religious practice. Until and unless they are divested of their stranglehold on places of worship, there is little chance of worship and there is little chance of their being restored as havens of spirituality. It is time somebody called the bluff of these money-grabbing parasites and made the houses of God fit places for deities and their worshippers.

# THE QUESTION OF REASON

Two news items in the foreign press have highlighted points of conflict between religious ritual and common sense. One comes from the city of Leicester in England. Leicester has a sizeable Muslim population with three mosques. As elsewhere in the Muslim world, the call to prayer (Azaan) went out five times a day, starting with the pre-dawn and ending well after children's sleeping time. Amplifiers were fitted in minarets to make sure that the muezzins were heard all over the city. Leicester has its own civic regulations, restricting sound to 70 decibels. The amplified call to prayer was 90 decibels. Non-Muslims protested and described the imposition as a nuisance. The local council met representatives of the Muslim community and Imams of the three mosques. A compromise was arrived at. The Azaans would not exceed 70 decibels and instead of the prescribed five, were reduced to three or four, which do not disturb peoples' sleep.

Why can't such sensible compromises be arrived at in India? Why should gurudwaras and temples wake up people at unearthly hours of the morning through kirtans and chantings over loudspeakers? Why should loudspeakers be permitted for use at all-night jagratas and prevent others from sleeping? Catch anyone like Imam Bukhari of Delhi's Jama Masjid agreeing to reduce the number of calls to prayer over microphones to under five, or using sound suppressors! In India, whenever religious rites and commonsense are in conflict, you can be sure that the rite, however irrational and irritating, will win.

The second case involves a more fundamental issue: how far can you permit a religious belief to put the life of a person in jeopardy? In this case it is a two-year-old child stricken with leukaemia. Doctors were of the opinion that if she did not get a blood transfusion, she would die. Her parents rejected medical advice on the grounds that belonging to a Christian sect known as Jehovah's Witnesses; they regarded blood transfusion as a sin. Jehovah's Witnesses are a sect started by one Charles Taze Russel of Pennsylvania in the 1870s. It was originally known as the Zion's Watch Tower Bible and Tract Society. You can see their members selling literature on the streets. Russel had predicted the return of Christ. Nothing happened. Christ did not bother to return to Earth and redeem it from evil. Russel also believed that taking others' blood into one's body was a sin as venal as rape. So his followers, who now number millions, would rather die than have somebody's blood pumped into them. They have every right to do so. But can they also impose their views on their children? Yes, say the elders of the Watch Tower Society—parents have the right to dictate to their children. No, said the High Court of London and ordered the child to be given blood transfusions. The parents abducted their two-year-old daughter from the hospital and flew to Cyprus, where they belonged. Fortunately, the authorities there agreed with the English and forced the parents to hand over the child. She received blood transfusions. And is alive.

We have similar situations arising in our country, as for instance, when a doctor performing an operation on a Sikh advises that he or she be shaved to avoid infection. Who then is to decide what is more important, adherence to religious belief or the life of an individual?

# WITH THE DEVOUT

While attending a seminar on religion and politics in Hyderabad, I was curious to know how religious or otherwise the seminarists were themselves. Of the thirty round the table, two declared themselves atheists and three agnostics. The remaining twenty-five, being Hindu, Muslim, Sikh and Parsi, did not think it necessary to say anything about their personal beliefs. Surprisingly, the only participants who somewhat aggressively asserted their religiosity were the four Christians. Two being foreign missionaries did not merit much attention; but the other two who were from Kerala and the youngest of the group went out of their way to proclaim their adherence to the church.

One of them, Babu Joseph, presented all seminarists a copy of his book, titled *Failure of Marxism: Victory of Jesus.*

## WITH THE DEVOUT

Joseph, who looked to be still in his twenties, is a professor and convenor of the Christian Liberation Movement. What they seek liberation from, I could only make out from a quotation from Saint Jude at the beginning of the book: 'For some godless men have slipped in unnoticed among us, who distort the message about the grace of our God, to excuse their immoral ways and reject Jesus Christ, our only Master and Lord.'

He was evidently after the Marxists. But to describe the godless as immoral is a gratuitous falsehood. Most men and women who deny God are to my knowledge more truthful, helpful, kinder and more considerate in their dealings with others than men of religion. What surprised me most was that the youngest and the comeliest of the participants, Thangam Jacob, was also immersed in Christianity. I decided to question her on the quiet during a coffee break. After I did so, she exposed me in front of the full assembly causing me much embarrassment. Of that later.

In the discussion several suggestions were made about the kind of religion that people should have and the limits to its ritualistic obeisance so that it did not become an imposition on others. One suggestion which no one took very seriously at the time when it was made by environmentalist Zafar Futehally who described himself as nominally a Muslim. He said, somewhat feebly I thought, that the religion of the future must be concerned with ecology. But the more I thought about it later, the more convinced I was that there was a lot to what he was saying. If we go on destroying our forests, polluting our streams with noxious wastes and fouling our air with poisonous fumes of petrol and coal, we are in fact destroying all that has been given to us—by God or some yet undiscovered power. No amount of temple-going, chanting mantras and recitations of scriptures is going to help us from committing mass hara-kiri.

We have had religious movements which, like the Secular Greens Movement in the West, were primarily concerned with the preservation of natural phenomenon, but they did not make the kind of impact they should have made. The outstanding example are the Bishnois who are fiercely dedicated to saving trees and animal life. I have enormous respect for all Bishnois, with the exception of Bhajan Lal, who I regard as the most mischievous politician of post-independent India. If the Bishnois could also include the preservation of human life (they have high incidence of crimes of violence among them), we would have a ecological religion going on a national scale.

Coming back to Thangam Jacob. As I said, I cornered her at a coffee-break and asked her: 'How does a young and pretty girl like you get so deeply involved in the clap-trap of religion?' A few minutes later she announced to

## WITH THE DEVOUT

the whole assembly, 'Mr Singh asked me why a young and beautiful girl like me had turned to religion. I told him that I was young and beautiful because my religion had made me so.' Moral: never make a private pass at a girl who publicly proclaims her adherence to God.

# A COMPETITION

One Sunday morning in Lahore, pre-monsoon showers had cleared the air of dust and a cool pleasant breeze was blowing. I rang up my friend Manzur Qadir (later foreign minister and chief justice of Pakistan) and suggested taking our families out to the Lawrence Gardens and giving children ice-creams at the Gymkhana Club. He agreed enthusiastically. We parked our cars at the Cosmopolitan Club. I had brought a red rubber ball with me. With our two families outings were enlivened with games and refresher courses on the names of trees and birds. The game was simple. Manzur or I tossed the ball into the branches of high trees, the children competed against each other in catching the ball as it bounced off the branches. So we went from one tree to another towards the Gymkhana Club. At one tree the ball got caught in a

## A COMPETITION

cleft of two branches. We hurled stones and sticks to dislodge it. After half an hour we gave up the ball as lost and proceeded to the club. We spent over an hour eating ice-creams and sipping coffee. Then we set back towards our cars. We passed under the tree and saw the red ball still lodged between the branches. I proclaimed very loudly, 'If that ball drops down on its own, I will believe there is a God.' A gentle gust of breeze shook the branches and the ball dropped directly into my hands.

'That should teach you a lesson!' said Manzur. 'God has now manifested His presence to you as you wished. It should silence your doubts forever.'

I was shaken but stood my ground. 'It was a mere coincidence,' I said. 'The only lesson it has taught me is that I should not treat serious problems like the existence of God as lightly as I do.'

God and religion were perennial topics of discussion between Manzur and myself. He was more concerned with spotting contradictions in the Judaic, Christian and Muslim scriptures than with God and His prophets. Neither of us observed the rituals of our respective faiths nor attached importance to religious dietary rules. But we never imposed our views on others. Both of us were described as agnostics but both retained our socio-religious identities. Though non-believers, he remained nominally Muslim, I nominally Sikh.

Discarding religious belief and practice, though hard enough, left many questions unanswered, most of all belief in the existence of God. Often in moments of solitude watching a star-studded sky, like everyone else, I asked myself. 'What is all this about? Where did it come from? Why? Where will I go when I die?'

Much as I thought about them, consulted books of wisdom of different religions and entered into dialogues with religious leaders, I found no answers. I refused to be bamboozled with words and formulas like 'the truth is within us only if we seek it'. Or 'the body dies but the soul is imperishable'. I came to the conclusion that they knew no more than I. And I knew there are no answers to these questions. We do not know where we come from, we know not the purpose of our lives on earth and we do not know where we go when we die. Instead of believing in fairy tales or Genesis and the Day of Judgement or equally baseless stories of reincarnation, why not be honest and admit I do not know?

I was confronted by examples of what has come to be known as the 'Unknown Hand'. There was the case of a man who fell on the tracks of the London underground railways as a train was approaching the platform. The train pulled up just as its wheels touched the man's legs. The driver swore he had not pulled the brakes. The emergency cord had been pulled by someone who could

## A COMPETITION

not possibly have seen the leg on the track. Who was it? They never found out. A somewhat similar incident happened with me. I bought a new Maruti car and took pains to park it under the shade of a mulberry tree outside my apartment. One hot afternoon I was in two minds about whether or not to go for a swim. A storm seemed to be building up and I was not sure whether it would be worth my while stepping out in the heat. Ultimately, something made me overcome my lethargy and take a chance. I had hardly gone a hundred yards when a dust storm swept across with great fury and tore a branch off the mulberry tree. It came crashing on the spot where I had parked my car. If I had been a minute late my new car would have been smashed. If I had been in it, I would not have been writing this piece. Was there an 'Unseen Hand' egging me on to leave for the club? It could very well have been a coincidence, a matter of good luck.

Thousands of people will tell you of similar events; like they missed a flight and the plane crashed or they happened to be outside their houses when an earthquake brought the roof down and killed others. An equal number of instances could be cited in which people lost their lives or were maimed because they undertook errands they need not have undertaken. This further led to the question: if there is a God, is he really Almighty as well as just? It is difficult to equate omnipotence with fair-mindedness because far too often, good, God-fearing people who have harmed no one suffers and the evil-minded who create havoc in other people's lives prosper in good health.

*Why Do Bad Things Happen To Good People?* is a well-argued little book by Rabbi Kushner whose young son was stricken by terminal cancer. His pleading in favour of the existence of a just, all-powerful God left me unconvinced. Among my closer friends of later years is Nirmala (Nimmy) Gupta, an attractive headmistress of a school in Mathura. She lost her only child, a boy in his twenties, in a car crash the day he had been confirmed in his job. 'I didn't asked for a child; God gave him to me. He gave the lad talent to write poetry. He was well loved by everyone. And suddenly one evening He takes him away from me. What had I done to deserve this cruel treatment?' This continues to be her theme many years after she lost her son: My response is: 'I do not believe in God and cannot be called upon to justify his actions.' Her only answer is a flood of tears.

There are millions of people for whom belief in the existence of God gives meaning to their lives. It is impossible to shake their faith. And not necessary to try to do so. When I first put my ideas in print in the *Indian Express*, ten-year-old Supriya, daughter of Rajmohan Gandhi, then resident editor in Madras and later Janata MP, wrote to me in Washington where I then happened to be. Supriya's letter ran somewhat as follows: 'Dear Uncle, I read your article in the *Express* this morning. So you do

## A COMPETITION

not believe in God! You are wrong. God exists. He comes to our garden everyday. He talks to my mummy and my daddy. He also talks to me. So there!' I was charmed by the child's outburst of faith in God's existence. I wrote back to her: 'Dear Supriya, I am glad to hear God visits your home regularly and He talks to your mummy, daddy and you. He does not talk to me. Please send me His telephone number so that I could also talk to Him.' Supriya did not bother to reply. I later met her father and asked him about his daughter. He sadly admitted that Supriya, then fifteen, had ceased to have dialogues with God and had turned agnostic.

The closer I get to the time of meeting my Maker, the more sceptic I become of his existence: Most people accept Voltaire's argument, 'We can scarcely believe that there can be a watch without a watch-maker'. Every effect must have a cause, they say. However, no one can get round the conundrum that if God is the cause and universe the effect, who or what was it that brought God into existence? What was the primary cause?

What should clinch the issue about God is that belief in his existence does not make a person a good man nor disbelief in his existence make him a bad man. I have known more saint-like people among agnostics than I have among God-fearing believers. In the personal religion I expound, there is no place for God.

# SIKHISM

In the life of every nation there comes a time when accepted values begin to be questioned. This is usually occasioned by a challenge from another set of values at variance with those formerly accepted. The conflict may result in compromise and the emergence of a new code of living incorporating principles common to both systems. Sometimes, the new code finds adherents who break away from their original loyalties to form a new community bound by allegiance to a new way of life. The Sikhs are an example of the emergence of a community with a communal consciousness fashioned out of new social norms.

For several centuries Indians accepted Hinduism as something ordained and immutable. From 780 AD began Muslim invasions from the north. The invaders' religion and way of life were the antithesis of whatever Hinduism stood for. Their religion was a simple set of dos and don'ts, most of them with direct bearing on matters of everyday life. A large part of the Koran consisted of rules on what a man may or may not eat and drink, how many wives he may marry, how to treat them and divorce them. The faith itself was brief and simple: that there was one God and Muhammad was his Prophet. The Koran was the word of God and what it said was law unto mankind. The Koran insisted on the unity of God in opposition to Hindu pantheism; it deified the iconoclast in a country of idol worshippers; it stood for the equality of men in a country ridden with caste distinctions; and it sanctioned pleasures of the flesh and palate in a country that preached the ascetic ideal.

For seven centuries Islam and Hinduism battled for supremacy. There were periods when Islam, with characteristic impatience, argued sword in hand. Hinduism, with characteristic resilience, withstood persecution and took the edge off the Islamic sword. By the fifteenth century, India had many million Muslims, but by then Muslims were observing caste distinctions, visiting Hindu temples, and generally accepting Hindu customs and conventions. Above all, they accepted the principles of religious tolerance. On the other side, the Hindus themselves recognized the superiority of the concept of the indivisibility of the Godhead, of the evils of caste and other unwholesome social customs. The stage was set for the emergence of a school of thought propagating a fusion of faiths based on principles common to Islam and Hinduism. This was the school of Bhakti philosophy.

Like the religious reformation in Europe, the Bhakti movement in India was basically a protest against religious dogma, ritual and intolerance. The propounders of Bhakti philosophy—Ramananda, Gorakhnath, Chaitanya, Kabir, Tulsidas, Vallabh and Namdev—taught that the form and place of worship were of little consequence and that basically Hinduism and Islam had the same values; only, the nomenclature was different. They evolved a form of religious poetry with a vocabulary that borrowed liberally from the sacred texts of both Hindus and Muslims. It had a spontaneity that appealed to the masses. All that the movement lacked was personal leadership and guidance. This was provided by Guru Nanak (1469–1539), the founder of the Sikh faith.

Guru Nanak, like the other Bhakti philosophers, was more concerned with spreading religious tolerance than with founding a new community. His teachings, however, fired the imagination of the Punjab peasantry and even during his lifetime a large number of followers gathered around him.

At first, they were merely known as his disciples (in

Sanskrit: shishya). Some time later, these disciples became a homogeneous group whose faith was exclusively the teachings of Nanak. The shishya became the 'Sikh' (corruption of the Sanskrit word).

Guru Nanak was content to be a teacher. He laid no claims to divinity or to kinship with God. He neither invested his writings with the garb of prophecy nor his words with the sanctity of a 'message'. His teaching was a crusade against cant and humbug in religion and his life was patterned by what he said. What he said was eminently well said, as his hymns are the finest in the Punjabi language. What he did was eminently well done, because his life was an example of his faith.

He ignored religious and caste distinctions and took as his associates a Muslim musician and a low-caste Hindu. He ridiculed such Hindu religious practices as giving importance to bathing in 'sacred' rivers, wearing 'sacred' threads and making offerings to dead ancestors. He personally went to the places of pilgrimage and demonstrated to worshippers their utter absurdity. Likewise, he went on pilgrimages to Muslim shrines and reprimanded priests who had made a trade of religion and transgressed the injunctions of the Koran. His success in efforts to bring Hindus and Muslims together was a personal one. He was acclaimed by both communities, and on his death they clamoured for his body—the Muslims wanted to bury him, the Hindus wanted to cremate him. Even today he is regarded in the Punjab as a symbol of harmony between the Hindus and the Muslims. A popular couplet describes him:

> Guru Nanak the King of Fakeers,
> To the Hindu a Guru, to the Muslims a Peer.

In fifty years of travel and teaching, Guru Nanak had attracted a following that could at best be described as a group dissenting from both, Hinduism and Islam. It was left to his successors to mould this group into a community with its own language and literature, religious beliefs and institutions, traditions and conventions.

Guru Nanak was followed by nine other Gurus. Succession was determined on the basis of finding a teacher most fitted to safeguard and develop the spiritual legacy left behind by Nanak. Hence, for two centuries, there was remarkable continuity in the functions of leadership. These years saw the consummation of the religious aspect of Sikhism. They also saw nascent Hindu nationalism grow to political power and pave the way to the setting up of a Sikh state. Of the ten Gurus, the second, Guru Angad; the fourth, Guru Ramdas; the sixth, Guru Hargobind; and the tenth, Guru Gobind Singh; were chiefly responsible for measures that fostered communal consciousness and welded the Sikhs into an independent community.

On the Hindu New Year's Day (13 or 14 April, depending on the leap year) in 1699, Guru Gobind Singh assembled his followers and initiated five, known as the Punj Piyaras (five beloved ones), into a new fraternity, which he named the Khalsa or 'the pure'. Of these five, one was a Brahmin, one a Kshatriya, and three belonged to the lower castes. They were made to drink out of the same bowl and given new names with the suffix 'Singh' (lion) attached to them. They swore to observe the 'Five Ks': to wear their hair and beard unshorn (kesh); to carry a comb in the hair (kungha); to wear a pair of shorts (kuchha); to wear a steel bangle on the wrist (kara); and to carry a sword (kirpan). The Khalsa were also enjoined to observe four rules of conduct (rahat): not to cut their hair; abstain from smoking tobacco and consuming alcoholic drinks; not to eat kosher meat; and refrain from carnal intercourse with Muslims. Ever since that day every Sikh youth, when he comes of age, is initiated into the Khalsa by the baptism (pahul) of the sword and the suffix 'Singh' is attached to his name. Thereafter he has no caste save one, the fraternity of the Khalsa.

The reason that prompted Guru Gobind Singh to introduce these forms and symbols has never been adequately explained. Neither he nor any of his contemporaries refer to the subject in their writings. Some of them are, however, intelligible in their historical background.

Guru Gobind Singh completed the religious facet of Sikhism. He turned an innocuous band of pacifists into armed crusaders. Those who did not accept his innovations of forms and symbols remained just Sikhs, usually described as Sahaj Dharis or 'the easygoing'; those who did became the Khalsa. Guru Gobind Singh lost all his four sons in the struggle against the Muslim rulers and declared the succession of Gurus at an end. The Sikhs were to look to the Adi Granth for spiritual guidance, which was henceforth to be the symbolic representation of the ten Gurus. Ceremonies and customs distinct from those of the Hindus were made current. Thus the Sikhs became a new community with an independent entity.

## The Sikh Religion

By legislative enactment a Sikh has been defined as 'one who believes in the ten Gurus and the Granth Sahib'. This definition is not exhaustive. There are people who call themselves Sikhs and yet do not believe in all the ten Gurus. There are others who believe that the line of Gurus continued after the tenth and follow the precepts of a living Guru.

Similarly, some Sikhs challenge the authenticity of

certain passages of the Granth Sahib, while others insist on including extraneous writing in it. Besides these Sikhs, there are numerous sub-sects distinguished by allegiance to one or the other Guru or claiming that the real Guru had been overlooked in deciding the succession. Despite these discrepant factors, it can be safely asserted that the belief in the ten Gurus and the authorized version of the Granth Sahib are the common basic factors of the Sikh faith, and they cover the vast majority of Sikhs. The only practical sectional division of the Sikh community is into the orthodox Khalsa and the clean-shaven Sahaj Dhari.

## The Concept of God

The Sikh religion, as enunciated in the scriptures, is a wholesome mixture of Islamic Sufi doctrines and Hindu mystic philosophy. It inculcates belief in the unity of God and equates God with truth. The preamble to the morning prayer Japji, which is recited as an introduction to all religious ceremonies and is known as the mool mantra, the basic belief, states:

> There is One God
> His Name is Truth.
> He is the Creator,
> He is without fear and without hate.
> He is beyond time Immortal,
> His Spirit pervades the universe.

> He is not born,
> Nor does He die to be born again,
> He is self-existent.
> By the guru's grace shalt thou worship Him.
>
> Before Time itself
> There was truth.
> When Time began to run its course
> He was the truth.
> Even now, He is the truth.
> Evermore shall truth persist.
>
> —Nanak

The tenth Guru, Gobind Singh, ventured farther into philosophic speculation in describing God as *akalpurukh* (timeless):

> Time is the only God,
> The primal and the final
> The Creator and the Destroyer.
> How can words describe him?
> God has no form or substance.
> He is *nirankar* (formless).
> Although He is beyond human comprehension,
> By righteous living one can invoke His grace.

In the first verse of the morning prayer, Japji, Guru Nanak said:

> Not by thought alone
> Can he be known,

## SIKHISM

Tho' one think a hundred thousand times
Not in solemn silence,
Nor in deep meditation.
Though fasting yields an abundance of virtue,
No! By none of these
Nor by a hundred thousand other devices
Can God be reached.
How then shall truth be known?
How the veil of false illusion torn?
O Nanak, thus runneth the writ divine.
The righteous path let it be thine.

The Sikh religion expressly forbids the worship of idols and emblems as Gods in no uncertain terms:

They that worship strange Gods
Cursed shall be their lives, cursed their habitations,
Poison shall be their food—each morsel.
Poisoned too shall be their garments.
In life for them is misery,
In life hereafter, hell.

—the third Guru, Amar Das

Some worship stones and on their heads they bear them,
Some the phallus-strung in necklaces wear its emblem.
Some behold their God in the South,
Some to the West bow their head,
Some worship images, others [are] busy praying to the dead.

> The world is thus bound in false ritual
> And God's secret is still unread.
> —the tenth Guru, Gobind Singh

Guru Nanak, while attending the evening service at a Hindu temple where a salver full of small oil lamps and incense was being waved in front of the idol before it was laid to rest for the night, composed this verse:

> The firmament is thy salver
> The Sun and Moon thy lamps,
> The galaxy of stars
> Are as pearls scattered.
> The woods of sandal are thy incense
> The forests thy flowers
> But what worship is this,
> O destroyer of Fear?

## The Guru or the Teacher

God being an abstraction, godliness is conceived more as an attribute than a concrete entity that can be acquired by a person or a thing. The way of acquiring godliness or salvation is to obey the will of God. The means of ascertaining God's will are, as in other theological systems, unspecified and subject to human speculation. They are largely rules of moral conduct, which are the basis of human society. Sikh religion advocates association with men of religion for guidance. Hence the importance of the guru or the teacher and the institution of discipleship.

Sikhs do not worship human beings as reincarnations of God. The Gurus themselves repeated that they were like other human beings and were on no account to be worshipped. Guru Nanak constantly referred to himself as the slave and servant of God. Guru Gobind Singh, who was the author of most of the Sikh practice and ritual, was conscious of the danger of having divinity imposed on him by his followers. He explained his mission in life:

> For though my thoughts were lost in prayer
> At the feet of Almighty God,
> I was ordained to establish a sect and lay down its rules.
> But whosoever regards me as Lord
> Shall be damned and destroyed.
> I am—and of this let there be no doubt—
> I am but a slave to God, as other men are,
> A beholder of the wonders of creation.

In another passage, he refuted claims to divinity and reincarnation made by others:

> God has no friends or enemies.
> He heeds no hallelujahs nor cares about cures.
> Being the first and timeless
> How could he manifest himself through those
> Who are born and die?

Godliness being the aim of human endeavour, the lives and teachings of the Gurus are looked upon as aids towards its attainment.

## The Granth Sahib

The compilation of the Granth Sahib was largely the work of the fifth Guru, Arjan Dev, and his disciple Bhai Gurdas. This compilation is known as the Adi Granth, the first scripture, to distinguish it from the Dasam Granth, the tenth scripture of the tenth Guru, Gobind Singh, which was compiled by his disciple Bhai Mani Singh.

By the ordinance of Guru Gobind Singh himself, the Adi Granth alone was given the status of the Holy Scripture as a symbolic representation of all the ten Gurus. His own Dasam Granth is read with reverence, but does not form part of ritual except at the ceremony of baptism.

The Adi Granth or the Granth Sahib contains the writings of the first five Gurus, the ninth Guru, Tegh Bahadur, and the couplet by Guru Gobind Singh. A fair part of the book, however, consists of the writings of Hindu and Muslim saints of the time, chiefly those of Kabir. The compositions of bards who accompanied the different Gurus are also incorporated in it.

The language used by the Sikh Gurus was Punjabi of the fifteenth and sixteenth centuries. Other writings are in old Hindi, Persian, Gujarati, Maharathi and other dialects of northern India. The whole work is set to the measure of classical Indian music with the number of the author Guru appearing first. All the Gurus used the literary nom de plume 'Nanak' at the end of each verse.

All the words appearing in each line are joined together, causing considerable confusion in the interpretation of the text. It is frequently impossible to tell whether there is one word or two words put together. Despite this, the Granth Sahib is a unique historical document. It is perhaps the only kind of writing of a scriptural nature that has preserved without embellishment or misconstruction the original writings of the religious leaders. It has saved the literary works of other poets of the time from the vagaries of human memory.

The Granth Sahib is the central object of Sikh worship and ritual. In all gurudwaras, copies of the Granth are placed under a canopy. The book itself is draped in cloth—usually embroidered. It is opened with prayer and ceremony each morning and in the evening. Worshippers appear before it barefooted and with their heads covered. They make obeisance by rubbing their foreheads on the ground before it. Offerings of money or food are placed on the cloth draping the book.

Sikh children are given a name beginning with the first letter appearing on the page at which the Granth may open. Sikh youth are baptized with the recitation of prayers in front of the Granth. Sikh couples are married to the singing of hymns from the Granth while they walk round it four times. Hymns are read aloud in a dying person's ears and on cremation they are chanted as the flames consume the body. Despite all this, the Granth Sahib is not like the idol in a Hindu temple or the cross in a Catholic church. It is the source and not the object of prayer or worship. Sikhs revere it because it contains the teachings of their Gurus. It is more a book of divine wisdom than the word of God.

## Pilgrimage

Sikhs neither believe in 'sacred' rivers and mountains nor do they pray to stone images. 'To worship an image, to make a pilgrimage to a shrine, to remain in a desert, and yet have the mind impure, is all in vain. To be saved, worship only the truth' (Nanak).

Although there are no places or occasions marked out for pilgrimage, Sikhs assemble on the birthday of the Gurus at their places of birth. The martyrdom of the fifth Guru, Arjan Dev, used to be celebrated at mammoth gatherings of Sikhs at Lahore and is today celebrated in Delhi and some other parts of India. The more important shrines—the birthplace of Guru Nanak (now in Pakistan), the site of Guru Arjan's execution at Lahore, the temples at Amritsar and Taran Taran (in Indian Punjab), the birthplace of Guru Gobind Singh at Patna and the site of his death in Nanded (in Maharashtra)—are visited by Sikhs at all possible times.

## Death and Life Hereafter

Sikhism accepts the Hindu theory of karma and life hereafter. It holds that there is rebirth after death and that the form of the re-created being is determined by his or her action in life; that a person may escape the vicious circle of death and rebirth by righteous living and thus achieve salvation:

> He who made the night and day,
> The days of the week and the seasons,
> He who made the breeze blow, the waters run,
> The fires and the lower regions,
> Made the earth—the temple of law.
> He who made creatures of diverse kinds
> With a multitude of names,
> Made this the law—
> By thought and deed be judged forsooth,
> For God is true and dispenseth truth.
> There the elect his court adorn,
> And God himself their actions honours.
> There are sorted deeds that were done and bore fruit
> From those that to action could never ripen.
> This, O Nanak, shall hereafter happen.
>
> —Nanak

## Society

Sikh tradition elevates society to the status of the lawgiver and the judge. The last Guru devised means by which the will of society could be ascertained and enforced. A resolution (mata) passed by elected representatives of the congregation (sangat) became a gurumata (the order of the Guru). A gurumata could even dispense with forms and conventions initiated by the Gurus themselves.

## Priesthood

The Sikhs do not have priests. All adults, irrespective of status or sex, are competent to perform religious ceremonies.

## The Caste System

The Sikh religion does not recognize the caste system. Guru Nanak chose a Muslim musician who would normally be beyond the pale of the caste system as a companion. Nanak's writings abound with passages describing as ungodly the conduct of those who condemn God's creatures to untouchability. For instance:

> There are ignoble amongst the noblest,
> And pure amongst the despised.
> The former shall thou avoid.
> And be the dust under the foot of the other.

The second Guru, Angad, said:

> The Hindus say there are four castes
> But they are all of one seed.
> 'Tis like clay of which pots are made
> In diverse shapes and forms-yet the clay is the same.
> So is the body of man made of five elements.
> How can one amongst them be high and another low?

Guru Gobind's first five disciples included three who were from the lower castes. With determined deliberation, he said that he would mix the four castes into one-like the four constituents of paan (betel), which when chewed, produce just one colour.

## Prayer

A feature of the Sikh religion, which is particularly striking, is its emphasis on prayer. The form of prayer is usually the repetition of the name of God and in chanting hymns of praise. This was popularized by the Bhakti cult, and Sikhism is its chief exponent today. The Sikh scriptures abound with the exhortation to repeat 'the True Name' as purification from sin and impious thoughts:

> As hands or feet besmirched with slime,
> Water washes white;
> As garments dark with grime
> Rinsed with soap are made light;
> So when sin soils the soul
> Prayer alone shall make it whole.

## ON RELIGION

> Words do not the saint or sinner make,
> Action alone is written in the book of fate,
> What we sow that alone we take;
> O Nanak, be saved or forever transmigrate.
>
> —Nanak

At the same time, there are positive injunctions against austere asceticism involving renunciation of society, celibacy and penance. All the Gurus led normal family lives and discharged secular functions as householders and as the spiritual mentors of their people. The concept of righteous living is meaningless except in the context of the community. There is constant reference to being in the world but not worldly. The ideal is to achieve saintliness as a member of society and to lead a spiritual existence with the necessary material requisites (raaj mein jog kamayo):

> Religion lieth not in the patched coat the Yogi wears,
> Not in the staff he bears,
> Nor in the ashes on his body.
> Religion lieth not in rings in the ears,
> Not in a shaven head,
> Nor in the blowing of the conch shell.
> If thou must the path of true religion see
> Amongst the world's impurities, be of impurities free.
>
> —Nanak

## Pacifism and the Use of Force

Sikh pacifism in religion and Sikh militarism present a contradiction, which can only be explained by a reference to history. A strictly pacifist faith is difficult to reconcile with a spartan military tradition, except through the formula that when the faith itself is threatened with extinction, force may be used to preserve it. This indeed was Guru Gobind Singh's explanation of the steps he took. In a Persian couplet, he said:

> Chu kar uz hama har heel te dar guzusht
> Halal ust burdan ba shamsheer dust.
> (When all other means have failed,
> it is righteous to draw the sword.)

It is possible that if the state of affairs in the Punjab had returned to a peaceful normality, the Sikh sword might have been sheathed and the gospel of Nanak, which preached peace and humanity, would have become symbolic of the Sikh faith. As it was, the period following Guru Gobind Singh was about the most turbulent known to Indian history. The decaying Mughal Empire took to making scapegoats of minorities to explain away its failures. There were pogroms of unprecedented savagery in which the small band of Sikhs was almost exterminated. Coincident with persecution within the country, came new Muslim invasions from the north, which destroyed any people or institution they deemed unIslamic. In such circumstances, martial traditions were forged which became an integral part of the Sikh life and gave the Sikhs the reputation of being a fighting people.

# THE DALAI LAMA

I asked for an audience with the Dalai Lama. I did not intend to question him about the Chinese occupation of his homeland—which to me is as immoral as the Russian occupation of Afghanistan, now fortunately at an end. Rulers of China are not bothered about political morality nor yield to pressures of world opinion. So there was no point my making the Dalai Lama talk of the offer of compromise settlement he had then made and its outright rejection by the Chinese. I was more intrigued by his claim that Buddhism is a more sophisticated religion than others as it strongly stresses rationality and is very modern in its sensitivity. He had gone on to say, 'For those types who want to follow a path of sceptical inquiry and reason, rather than a path of faith, Buddhism may prove useful.' Buddha himself said, 'Do not believe in anything merely because I said it. Be like an analyst buying gold, cutting and burning the substance to test it in every way. Accept it only when it meets the full criteria of reason, and when it proves to be of benefit to you.' That kind of attitude is compatible with modern scientific outlook.

I arrived in Dharamsala where the Dalai Lama is in residence since his exile from Tibet. The upper part of the mountain range known as McLeodganj has become a little Tibet in India: Tibetan schools, libraries, a medical institute, a separate township for 1,500 children, temples, and over fifty restaurants serving Tibetan food. You hear more Tibetan spoken than the local Pahadi dialect of Kangra.

Before I tell you of my question-and-answer session, let me tell you of the Dalai Lama's background. He was one of sixteen children of a peasant family of eastern Tibet of which only seven survived their infancy. At the age of two he was picked up by the national committee charged with the duty of finding the incarnation of the 13th Dalai Lama who had died in 1933. Two years later he was brought to Lhasa, proclaimed His Holiness Tenzin Gyatso, the 14th Dalai Lama. However odd this system of locating successors may sound to sceptical ears, it has an enormous advantage over other political or social systems: from childhood a boy is trained to take over the responsibilities of a spiritual and secular leader of his people. He does not have to be the eldest son of a king to become the Prince of Wales nor the son of a president or a prime minister to be the heir presumptive. By the time he takes over his responsibilities, he is fully acquainted with his job. Tibetan Buddhism does not separate politics from religion. The 14th Dalai Lama is Tibet's secular and spiritual monarch.

I waited my turn to be received. A group of monks came out with a boy of five with his head shaved. He had been discovered as a reincarnation of another lama and initiated by His Holiness. A German couple waiting before us in the queue were ushered in. Fifteen minutes later we were asked to go in. The Dalai Lama stood outside his reception room—a tall, powerfully built man wreathed in smiles of welcome. We presented the traditional silk scarfs, shook hands and were escorted to our seats.

'Your Holiness, I am not going to ask you about politics. My questions will be on matters of religion. I am an agnostic and they may sound impertinent. I ask to be forgiven before I begin.'

He laughed uproariously and took my hand. 'In that case I can relax. I have to be very careful about politics: you may ask what you like.'

I had my list of questions ready: How did life originate? Is there a God? If so, why is there so much injustice and wickedness in the world? Are there rewards and punishments for good or evil deeds done in life? What is death—the destruction of body and mind or only the body? Is there a life hereafter or a rebirth after death?

My first question to the Dalai Lama was his view of the origin of life on our planet. Did he accept the Judeo-Christian-Muslim belief of it being created by a Supreme God? Or did he accept Darwin's Theory of Evolution: not from divine but natural causes—from amoeba to fish to land creatures, birds, mammals, monkeys down to man? There is also the intermediate theory put forward by Hinduism and its off-shoots (Jainism, Buddhism, Sikhism) of order emerging from chaos by the intervention of divinity in the form of a Creator, Preserver and Destroyer.

'As a Buddhist as well as personally I do not accept the theory of a divine Creator of life,' replied the Dalai Lama. 'The real creator is one's own mind. The universe and all its galaxies were created or happened at a certain period of time.' He was not precise about the time or the causes which brought it about but once life evolved in its different manifestations, their forms were determined by karmas—deeds. He then added: 'Buddhist scriptures maintain that certain sections of humanity are different from others. In Tibetan mythology there is a story that the Tibetan race came into being through the mating of a monkey and an ethereal being.' You can see an element of Darwinism in this legend which describes the evolution of a race from an earthy and a celestial being.

The Dalai Lama also accepted the possibility of virgin birth. 'In my generation and even earlier there were instances of women who had not been near a man conceiving. Conception was preceded by strange dreams. The offspring of such virgin births were extremely powerful and mentally advanced beings.'

The Dalai Lama repeated that he did not accept the notion of a creator God. Life came into being through a mysterious and subtle energy. Some people were more evolved than others; the greater majority evolved as Darwin spelt out in his Theory of Evolution.

I did not fully comprehend his line of argument, as at times for loss of the right word he broke into Tibetan and had to be translated into English. I went on to my next question: 'Even if you do not credit God with creation, do you believe in God as an omnipotent and compassionate reality?'

'God in the Christian sense and as some other religions see it as someone Supreme and Almighty, we Buddhist do not accept,' said the Dalai Lama categorically.

'What then do you accept as God?' I asked him. He paused a long time. I prodded him further: 'Do you regard Him as compassionate?'

My question had to be translated into Tibetan before

he replied. 'You know the three pillars of our faith, the Buddha, the Dhamma (Dharma) and the Sangha (Community).'

I nodded.

'For us the Buddha is a higher being, one who has reached the highest stage (of evolution). His mind has been completely purified of all dross. The Buddha was not there from the very beginning; he became one after he had purified his mind, rid it of negative thoughts and ignorance till they totally disappeared.'

He elucidated his views further. 'He was very much like ourselves to start with. Like students in a class are equals when they start. As they learn, differences develop. Some acquire knowledge and become teachers. There is a lot of difference between a teacher and a student. We regard the Sakyamuni as a teacher not a Creator.'

My next question was based on the wrong assumption that the Dalai Lama would accept the existence of a creator, an all-powerful and just God. He did not. Nevertheless, I put it to him: 'Can you explain why there is so much injustice and cruelty in the world? Why do bad things happen to good people?'

The great stumbling block in the way of people who believe that God is both all-powerful as well as just is the prevalence of injustice and cruelty in the world. Why, for instance, have a God-fearing people like the Tibetans had to flee their country and 95,000 of them forced to live in exile in India? I put the dilemma to the Dalai Lama.

'We Buddhist believe in Karma,' he replied. 'Life is a continuous circle without a beginning or an end. Deeds done in one life, one's Karmas, determine one's fate in the next. Even in one's lifetime bad deeds produce bad effects.'

I was not convinced. 'Does your Holiness believe that the entire Tibetan people are being punished for deeds done in the previous lives?'

'Yes,' he responded without pause. 'There is individual Karma and common Karma. The present travails of the Tibetan people are due to both kinds of Karmas. Some for acts done by individuals at some time or place, now come together in common suffering.'

I did not buy the explanation. 'Your Holiness, I am a sceptic and an agnostic. I find no rational basis for accepting the theory of Karma and rebirths nor the system of rewards and punishments in heaven or hell. There is no scientific basis for accepting one or the other.'

The Dalai Lama laughed heartily. 'Scientific proof is what you want?' he asked. 'But certain things are beyond scientific proof. I have many thoughts going on in my mind, it is difficult to give scientific explanations for them. Every particle of the body and mind is changing all the time, but none of these changes can be measured by computers.'

I protested. 'Since you cannot adduce rational, scientific explanations for certain phenomenon, wouldn't it be more truthful to say "I don't know"? As for me, I go further and say not only I do not know the answers, nobody else knows them either.'

The Dalai Lama stuck to his ground. 'There are two kinds phenomena. One are provable by science; the second are beyond the realm of scientific proof. But that does not mean they do not exist. Only scientists do not as yet know about them.'

'Then why not say that till such time as the scientists have found out we withhold our judgement.'

'I agree. Buddhism is quite clear on the subject: investigate till you find out the right answers. Do not accept anything and take it for granted. The Buddha himself said, "Do not accept anything said by me out of respect for me. If it does not appeal to you, reject it."'

'Would you extend the scope of inquiry to basic Buddhist beliefs like Karma and life hereafter?' I asked him.

'Yes,' replied the Dalai Lama. 'If scientists can prove that there is no next life, we Buddhists will accept it.'

'Why then persist in propagating unprovable theories till we can prove them?' I persisted.

The Dalai Lama pondered over the question for a while before replying. 'If you don't accept the past or the future, you are only left with this life. You can trace it back to your parents, grandparents back to millions of years back to the amoeba and further back to empty space. Then you either accept the Almighty creator and land yourself in more contradictions and more questions. How did it happen? The Buddhist concept of a beginningless beginning, continuity of consciousness and Karma, coming and going from to time till the space article came into existence avoids these contradictions.'

We went on to other questions, like why wickedness so often triumphs over goodness, why innocent people suffer while evil people prosper. Instead of the half hour allotted to me, the interview went on to one hour and a half. The tape ran out. As did his secretary's patience. There were other visitors waiting to see the Dalai Lama.

We took our leave. I was exhilarated by being with him. He extended that aura of goodwill, cheerfulness and crystal-clear honesty that envelops you long after you have left his presence. The Nobel Prize committee has done well in awarding him the peace prize because he is a man of peace. He has suffered many wrongs but never uttered an angry word in protest. He has brought solace to millions of people who are troubled by the way the world is going today.

# A MONK WITH GOOD TASTE

As often happens to me, when I go out in quest of the spiritual, I stumble on the earthly and find myself fully absorbed in it. My mission to Dharamsala was to seek an audience with the Dalai Lama, ask him questions on God, reincarnations, the purpose of life, suffering, death and life hereafter. But the first thing I did after unpacking at the Hotel Tibet was to visit the Tibetan Emporium next door. Apart from carpets, woollens and other artifacts, it also had books. 'Poetry,' I asked the lady attendant, 'preferably modern Tibetan poetry translated into English.'

'I have only one,' she replied in impeccable English. (Tibetans seem to have the gift of tongues; Urdu, Hindi, Hindustani or English, they speak it without a trace of an accent.) 'It is the compilation of one by our Dalai Lama,' she said as she handed me a slim volume: *Songs of the Sixth*

## A MONK WITH GOOD TASTE

*Dalai Lama,* complied by K. Dhondup. I took it as there was nothing else available. I expected it would be about the Lord Buddha, his various manifestations, the Four Noble Truths, the Eightfold Path to Nirvana—and that kind of thing. I was pleasantly surprised to find that it was about love, fornication, and the pleasures of the tavern flowing with chhung—rice wine. The institution of the wandering sanyasi adept in the art of seduction and performing great sexual feats also existed among those recognized as reincarnations of the great Sakyamuni who renounced sex and family life in early youth.

'Tsanyang Gyatso, the sixth Dalai Lama, remains a timeless enigma in the annals of the Dalai Lamas of Tibet,' writes Gyatso Tsering, director of the Tibetan Archives at Dharamsala. The institution of the Dalai Lama began in the 15th century with the recognition of Gedun Drupa as the first earthly manifestation of the Bodhisatva—Avalokiteshwara. In the 17th century, Tibet produced a remarkable leader, the Desi (regent or peshwa) named Sonam Choepel who succeeded in unifying Tibet under the fifth Dalai Lama, Ngawang Lobsang Gyatso. The Dalai Lama died in 1682. The Desi kept the news of his death secret for fifteen long years till he discovered the reincarnation and successor in the person of the sixth Dalai Lama who was enthroned in 1697. He was a gifted child, scholarly and of a poetic bent of mind. But he also loved the great out-of-doors activities. He liked archery and designing buildings. He refused to be disciplined and be bound down by vows of celibacy. For him it was the monastery and prayer by day time; taverns, drink, songs of love and pretty Tibetan maidens at night:

> Even if meditated upon,
> The face of my lama comes not to me
> But again and again comes to me
> The smiling face of my beloved.

He admitted defeat in pursuit of the spiritual:

> If I could meditate upon the dhamma,
> As intensely as I must on my beloved
> I would certainly attain enlightenment
> Surely, in this one lifetime.

And again:

> If the maiden will live forever
> The wine will flow, evermore
> The tavern is my haven
> With wine, I am content.

Inevitably he fell out with the regent. The regent was captured and beheaded in 1706. The sixth Dalai Lama's reign also came to an end the same year. He was forcibly taken away to China—and disappeared or was murdered. His last message was to a lama friend:

## A MONK WITH GOOD TASTE

> White Crane!
> Lend me your wings,
> I will not fly far;
> From Lithang, I shall return.

In the last line Tibetans read the message that the seventh Dalai Lama would soon be discovered.

Tsanyang Gyatso was not moved about his sexual prowess:

> Never have I slept without sweetheart
> Nor have I spent a single drop of sperm.

The sex act, as in the case of Krishna, was a tantric exercise in whom the bindus' latent powers were not to be wasted by being spent. If the body hoarded semen, the mind dwelt more intensely on the pleasure of sex.

> I went to my teacher, with devout filled
> To learn of the Lord Buddha
> My teacher taught, but what he escaped;
> For my mind was full of compassion,
> Full of that Compassionate One who loves me,
> She has stolen my mind.
> He was adept in the art of arousing
> Sweetheart awaiting me in my room
> Yielding tenderly her sweet body
> Has she come to cheat me
> And disrobe me of my virtues

> With fair damsels came wine:
> If the maiden will live forever
> The wine will flow, evermore
> The tavern is my haven
> With wine, I am content.

It is incredible that in a highly conservative and religion-oriented society like the Tibetan, it is the iconoclastic sixth Dalai Lama who remains the great favourite.

# GURU NANAK

On the night of the full moon in the month of Baisakh in the Samvat version—Mehervan's *Janam Sakhi*, on the life of Guru Nanak—Tripta, the wife of Mehta Kalian Das Bedi of Talwandi Rae Bhoe, was in labour. Three-quarters of the night had passed. The morning star shone bright in the eastern sky; it was the hour of early dawn when she was delivered of her second child, a son.

Nanak's birth was thus on 15 April 1469. However, in order to continue an old tradition, the event is celebrated on the full-moon night in the month of November. As to the place of his birth, it is thought that the name Nanak was given to the child because he was born in the house of his maternal grandparents, or nankey, which was either in Karma Kacha or Chalewal, two villages in the district of Lahore.

Nanak was a precocious child, smiling and sitting up in early infancy. When he was only five years old, people noticed that he did not play with other boys but spoke words of wisdom well beyond his years.

The people's reactions were interesting. Whosoever heard him, Hindu or Muslim, was certain that God spoke through the little boy—and this belief grew stronger as Nanak grew older.

At the age of seven Nanak was taken to a pandit to be taught. Nanak apparently turned the tables on his teacher and his discourse with his teacher is the subject of a beautiful hymn in Raga Sri. According to Nanak: 'The only real learning is the worship of God; the rest is of no avail, and wisdom devoid of the knowledge of the Creator is but the noose of ignorance about one's neck. He that repeats the name of the Lord in this world, will reap his reward in the world to come.

'Do you know how and why men come into this world and why they depart? Why some become rich and others poor? Why some hold court while others go begging door to door—and even of the beggars why some receive alms while others do not? Take it from me, O pandit, that those who have enjoyed power and ease in this life and not given praise to the Lord will surely be punished—just as the dhobi beats dirty clothes on slabs of stones, so will they be beaten; just as an oilman grinds oilseeds to extract oil will they be ground; just as the miller crushes grain between his millstones will they be crushed. On the other hand, those that are poor and those that have to beg for their living, who spend their lives in prayer will receive their honour and reward in the divine court of justice.

'He that has fear of God is free from all fears. But monarch or commoner, he that fears not God will be reduced to dust and be reborn to suffer the pangs of hell. That which is gained by falsehood becomes unclean. The only truth is God. Our only love should be for God who is immortal; why love those that will perish—son, wife, power, wealth, youth—all are subject to decay and death' (Mehervan: *Janam Sakhi*).

A year later Nanak was sent to the village mosque to learn Arabic and other subjects. Here, too, Nanak astounded his teacher: The mullah wrote down the Arabic alphabet from 'alif' to 'yea'. Nanak at once mastered the writing and the pronunciation of the letters, and within a few days had learnt arithmetic, accounting and everything else the mullah could teach. The mullah marvelled: 'Great God! Other children have been struggling for ten years and cannot tell one letter from another, and this child has by Thy grace learnt all within a matter of days' (Mehervan: *Janam Sakhi*).

Nanak was a moody child and often refused to speak to anyone for days on end. He wandered about the woods absorbed in observing the phenomena of nature: the advent of spring with its bees and butterflies; the searing heat of summer that burned up all vegetation, followed by the monsoon which miraculously restored life and turned the countryside green; the ways of the birds and beasts of the jungle. All this mystery baffled young Nanak's mind and he began to ponder over the character of the Creator, Preserver and Destroyer—and to question the efficacy of rituals, both Hindu and Muslim.

When he was only nine, Nanak demanded of the Brahmin priest who had come to invest him with the sacred thread, the janeu: 'Do the Brahmins and Kshatriyas lose their faith if they lose their sacred thread? Is their faith maintained by their thread or by their deeds?'

Nanak was the despair of his parents. He refused to do any kind of work. If he was sent to graze cattle, he let them stray into people's fields; if he was given money to do trade, he would give it away to the poor and the hungry. He was saved from the wrath of his father by his mother and sister—and by the village folk who bore witness to the many miracles they had seen Nanak perform.

At the age of sixteen Nanak was married to Sulakhni, daughter of Mul Chand Chona of Batala. They had two sons, Sri Chand and Lakhmi Das, and perhaps a daughter or daughters who died in infancy. Family life did not divert Nanak's attention for too long. His moods would suddenly descend upon him, and he would remain silent for many days and then become argumentative on subjects such as God, man, death, rituals and moral values. And he remained as indifferent to making a living as he had been before he became a husband and father.

One evening in July (Mehervan: *Janam Sakhi*), the skies over Talwandi were darkened by black monsoon clouds and it began to pour. At night the sky was rent with flashes of lightning and there was a fearful crash of thunder. Nanak began to sing hymns in praise of the Lord. His mother came to him and said, 'Son, it is time you had some sleep.' Just then the cuckoo called 'peeoh, peeoh', and Nanak replied, 'Mother, when my rival is awake, how can I sleep?'

It became evident to the people that it would not be long before Nanak took the hermit's path in search of truth and once, when a group of holy men happened to pass through Talwandi on their way to a pilgrimage, Nanak's mother expressed her apprehensions.

'I know,' she said, 'that one of these days you too will be leaving me to go on a pilgrimage. I do not complain but would like to know what is gained by going to holy places.'

'Nothing,' replied Nanak categorically. 'It is in our own body that we have to build our temples, free our minds from the snares of maya, renounce evil deeds and give praise to our Maker. This is as good as going to bathe in the sixty-eight holy places of pilgrimage.'

'Then tell these holy men that they pursue the path of error,' said Nanak's mother. 'Tell them that God can be found in their own houses.'

'Let each one find his own path,' replied Nanak. 'Why should I worry my head about their methods?'

The beauty of the woodland in spring cast its usual spell. But, for Nanak, the beauty was now tinged with anguish for he needed to know the truth of the reality that did not change with the seasons.

It was springtime. The trees were in new leaf; many wild shrubs were in flower. The woods around Talwandi were a beauteous sight. Young men of his village came to him and said, 'Nanak, it is spring. Come with us and let us behold the wonders of nature.'

'The month of Chaitra,' said Nanak, 'is the most beautiful of the twelve months of the year, because all is green and every living thing seems to blossom into fullness. But my heart does not rejoice at the sight of the blossoming of nature until it is blessed with the name of the Lord. We must first subdue our ego, sing praises of the Lord and then our hearts too will be fragrant.'

'We do not understand what you say,' they protested. 'We want to tell you that in the woods the trees are so green that we cannot find words to describe them; there are varieties of flowers whose beauty is beyond the speech of man; there are fruits whose lusciousness is beyond praise; and beneath them the shade is cool and fragrant. You should see these things with your own eyes.'

'The Lord's grace,' says Nanak, 'gave the trees their new foliage. His decrees covered them with blossoms of great beauty and filled their fruits with sweet nectar. When they have their foliage the Lord makes their shade cool and fragrant. I have such foliage in my own heart with similar flowers, fruit and cool shade, and people seek shelter under it.'

'The great God has given us eyes to see, ears to hear and a mouth to speak and eat the corn that grows. Why has He given us these things?'

'He has given you eyes not merely to gape at the woods but to behold His creation and marvel at it; ears to hear godly counsel; the tongue to speak the truth. Thereafter, whatever you receive is your true wealth and sustenance.'

The young men did not understand all that Nanak said. They tried once more to persuade him to come out with them. 'Spring comes but once a year and nature dons its garb of green but once. Then comes the fall. Trees lose their foliage and the woods are barren of beauty. If you want to see nature at its best, see it in the month of Chaitra.'

'Months and seasons ever come and go and come

again,' replied Nanak. 'Trees and bushes attain foliage in one season, lose it in another and once again become green when the season turns. The lesson for you is to see that those who do good acts reap the fruit of good action, and those who do evil, wither and die; those who take the name of the Lord ever have spring in their hearts. The grape only receives its juice during the monsoon but the good man receives his reward at all times of the year and all times of the day and night. Human birth is the springtime of the cycle of birth, death and rebirth; it is the time for you to plant the seed of good action and reap its fruit in life thereafter; in this, do not tarry.'

As Nanak grew even more detached from the ties of living, he took no notice of his wife or children, of his goods or of the people about him. His life became one of prayer, almsgiving, ablution and the seeking after knowledge: naam, daan, isnaan and gyaan. Lust, anger and pride fell away as Nanak's heart was filled with truth and blessed contentment. Nanak lived in this state 'like one drunk' for some years till his sister, Nanaki, now married, took the situation in hand. She persuaded her husband, Jai Ram, to invite her brother over to Sultanpur, where they lived, and get him employment with his master, Nawab Daulat Khan Lodhi.

Nanak went to Sultanpur accompanied by a family servant, a Muslim named Mardana, who was to become his closest companion. Mardana, the *Janam Sakhi* tells us, came from the brewer caste, and was a gifted musician. Mardana played the rabab and also sang hymns.

Nawab Daulat Khan Lodhi was impressed with the integrity of his new storekeeper and accountant. Nanak would not accept bribes from agents and refused to follow the corrupt practices of his predecessors. The people in Sultanpur could not stop praising Nanak.

In Sultanpur, Nanak organized his daily life in an ideal manner. Every evening he and Mardana would sing hymns before retiring to bed. Nanak would wake up while it was still dark and, after a dip in the river close by, sing hymns with the coterie of his followers. After this, at the appointed hour, Nanak would go to the court of the Nawab and apply himself to his work.

Though he won the approbation of his employer and those he dealt with, Nanak was unhappy.

'This has been suddenly put around my neck like a noose,' he said. He began to say to himself that if he had to serve anyone, wouldn't it be wiser to serve his own Master who is within him instead of the person without? It is all very well to seek knowledge and wisdom but one cannot escape the noose of maya without sowing the seeds of good actions. One cannot earn wages without service and it is the love of the wage which stands in the way of renunciation. Why not then serve the great Master who is the Lord of all? Nanak postponed his decision with the thought: 'I, Nanak, am no better than others; others are no worse than I; what the Lord wills, Nanak will honour and obey' (Mehervan: *Janam Sakhi*).

It was, however, clear that the time of decision was at hand.

Nanak's days were spent in noting down receipts and expenses. At the end of the day he added up the totals to make sure they tallied with the accounts. He often had to work late into the night adding up his figures under the light of the lamp. One night he got angry with himself and threw away his pen and account books. He asked himself, 'Why have I got involved in these affairs and forgotten my Maker? Am I destined to spend my days and nights writing accounts? It is a vast net in which I find myself caught; if I let the days go by, the noose will close tighter around me. If I have to burn the midnight oil, it should be for something worthwhile.'

Nanak pondered over these things late into the night and, instead of returning home, went to the stream to bathe. He prayed, 'Lord send me a guru, a guide who will show me the path that leads to Thy mansion.'

That very night God revealed Himself to Nanak. Nanak prayed fervently and begged the Lord to forgive him and remove him from the world which had so ensnared him. The Lord asked Nanak, 'Why are you so agitated? You have done no wrong.'

'I have let my mind turn from Thee,' replied Nanak, 'to the petty trifles of the world.'

'Your errors have I forgiven. The maya that you complain of is also a part of Me. What you see is but its shadow.'

'Lord, destroy in me the longing for worldly gain.'

'Nanak you shall no more crave for worldly gain. I am pleased with you. On you be My blessing' (Mehervan: *Janam Sakhi*).

The mystic experience that finally made Nanak take up his mission is put at different times and is variously described. The incident took place in August 1507 on the third night before the full moon.

The moon had set (says the *Janam Sakhi*), but it was dark and the stars still twinkled in the sky when Nanak, followed by Mardana, went to the river. Nanak took off his kurta and dhoti and stepped into the stream.

He closed his nostrils and ducked into the water. He did not come up. Mardana waited a while and then, panicking, ran up and down the riverbank crying for Nanak. A strange voice rose from the waters saying, 'Do not lose patience.'

Mardana, however, ran back to Sultanpur and sobbed out his story. A great commotion took place in the town because Nanak was loved by all—Hindus and Muslims, the rich and the poor. When Daulat Khan Lodhi heard of the mishap, he was most distressed. 'Friends,' he said, 'Nanak was a man of God. Let us dredge the river and rescue his corpse.'

While the people of Sultanpur were dredging the river, Nanak was conducted into the presence of God.

The Almighty gave him a bowl of milk. 'Nanak, drink this bowl,' He commanded. 'It is not milk as it may seem; this is nectar (amrit). It will give thee power of prayer, love of worship, truth and contentment.'

Nanak drank the nectar and was overcome. He made another obeisance. The Almighty then blessed him. 'I release thee from the cycle of birth, death and rebirth; he that sets his eyes on you with faith will be saved; he that hears your words with conviction will be helped by Me; he that you forgive will be forgiven by Me. I grant thee salvation. Nanak go back to the evil world and teach men and women to pray (naam), to give in charity (daan) and to live cleanly (isnaan). Do good to the world and redeem it in the age of sin (Kaliyuga)' (Mehervan: *Janam Sakhi*).

At dawn, three days later, on the full moon in August, Nanak re-emerged from the Bein. Nanak was thirty-six years old and now a changed and determined man. While the people clamoured around him acclaiming him as a new messiah, he paid no heed. 'What have I to do with men like these!' he said to himself. He gave away all he had to the poor. He even cast off his clothes, keeping for himself only a loincloth. He left his home and joined a band of hermits.

Soon people began expressing themselves loudly. 'Nanak was a sensible man,' some said, 'but now he has lost his head.' 'He is stricken with the fear of the Lord,' said others, 'and is no longer himself.' 'Something in the river has bitten him,' the rest were convinced, and took to calling him 'mad, bewitched'.

'It is the Lord who has possessed me and made me mad,' explained Nanak. 'If I find merit in the eyes of my Lord, then will I have justified my waywardness.'

'Nanak, you are a different person today from what you were!' the people exclaimed. Tell us the path you intend to take. We only know of two ways—one of the Hindus and the other of the Mussalmans.'

'There is no Hindu, there is no Mussalman,' replied Nanak.

'You talk in cryptic language,' they said. 'In this world we understand the two ways—of Hinduism and of Islam.'

'There are no Mussalmans, there are no Hindus,' repeated Nanak (Mehervan: *Janam Sakhi*).

Nanak spent another two years in and around Sultanpur before he forsook the habitations of men and took to the forests and solitude. The faithful Mardana was his sole companion. He took on a strange dress: a cloth cap, a long cloak worn by Muslim mendicants, a beggar's bowl, staff and prayer mat. When asked why he wore this outlandish garb, Nanak replied, 'I am dressed like a clown for the amusement of my Master. If my apparel pleases Him, I will be happy.'

Nanak's first journey took him eastwards to Hindu centres of pilgrimage. His biographies have fabricated many incidents based on Nanak's hymns—many of which depict the Guru's love for nature.

One day, Nanak and Mardana, while travelling, espied a flock of swans flying overhead. Nanak was bewitched and began to run after them with his eyes fixed on the birds (Mehervan: *Janam Sakhi*). Mardana followed him. The flock descended in a field and let Nanak approach them without showing any sign of fear—for Nanak was a man of God, who harmed no one. Nanak admired the birds, their long slender necks, their luminous dark eyes and their silver-white plumage. He wondered whether these birds—who spanned the heavens—had ever cast their eyes on their Maker. Why, he asked himself, should such beautiful birds wander restlessly across the continents, from Khorasan in Central Asia to Hindustan and back again to Khorasan? He blessed the swans and bade them godspeed on their journey.

Another hymn illustrates the political and social

conditions of the time through picturing an incident that occurred in the suburbs of the capital city, Delhi.

The city was at the time ruled by a bloodthirsty Pathan king (Ibrahim Lodhi). Nanak's fame had preceded him and large crowds of citizens, sightseers and seekers after truth, Muslims as well as Hindus, came to see him. Near Nanak's camp was a place where beggars and mendicants were fed free of charge by the wicked king. The people told Nanak of their king's evil ways and how he expiated his sins by feeding beggars.

Nanak spoke to them, 'Listen ye children of God! This charity of the king is of no consequence; it is the act of a blind man stumbling in the dark. He is worse than a blind man because even if his eyes lose their light, a blind man can hear and speak and comprehend, but one who has lost his mind has lost all. What avail is the giving of alms to one who sins by day and gives in charity at night? A stone dam can hold the flood but if the dam bursts you cannot repair the breach by plastering mud. Evil is like the flood, the stone dam like faith. If faith weakens, the dam will give way and the flood will sweep all before it. Its force is then so great that no boat nor boatman dare embark on it to save its victims. Then nothing abides save the name of the Lord' (Mehervan: *Janam Sakhi*).

We do not know how long Nanak stayed in Delhi. He proceeded to Haridwar on the Ganges. It was apparently at a time of some religious festival when large crowds had turned up to bathe in the 'holy' river. Mardana was very impressed with the sight and said to Nanak: 'What a lot of good people there are in the world! They must be genuinely desirous of improving themselves; that is why they come on a pilgrimage.'

Nanak was not so impressed by the sight of the people 'washing away their sins' by the ritual of bathing. 'Only a bullion dealer can tell the difference between the genuine and the counterfeit,' he replied, 'and at this place there is no bullion dealer.'

Nanak and Mardana stayed at Haridwar for some time in order to be present at the Baisakhi fair. It was on this occasion that an incident, that made Nanak famous, took place.

There was a large crowd bathing in the river. Nanak saw them face eastwards and throw palmfuls of water to the sun. Nanak entered the stream and started throwing water westwards.

'In the name of Rama!' exclaimed the shocked pilgrims, 'who is this man who throws water to the west? He is either mad or a Mussalman.' They approached Nanak and asked him why he offered water in the wrong direction. Nanak asked them why they threw it eastwards to the sun.

'We offer it to our dead ancestors,' they replied.

'Where are your dead ancestors?'

'With the gods in heaven.'

'How far is the abode of the gods?'

'Forty-nine crore kos from here.'

'Does the water get that far?'

'Without doubt! But why do you throw it westwards?'

Nanak replied, 'My home and lands are near Lahore. It has rained everywhere except on my land. I am therefore watering my fields.'

'Man of God, how can you water your fields near Lahore from this place?'

'If you can send it forty-nine crore kos to the abode of the gods, why can't I send it to Lahore which is only a couple of hundred kos away!'

The people were abashed at this reply. 'He is not mad,' they said. 'He is surely a great seer' (Mehervan: *Janam Sakhi*).

A large number of Hindu pilgrims who had foregathered at Haridwar became disciples of the guru. He stayed on there after the Baisakhi festival, preaching to the people.

'The most precious gift of God is human birth because it is by reason and responsible action as human beings that we can get out of the vicious circle of life, death and rebirth, and attain salvation. One must abolish duality in order to be a complete devotee.'

'And how does one overcome duality?' they asked.

'By faith in the One. By hearing and speaking of the One. By never abandoning belief in Him. By austerity, truth, restraint in his heart' (Mehervan: *Janam Sakhi*).

From Haridwar, Nanak and Mardana proceeded to Prayag (Allahabad) where the rivers Jamuna and Saraswati join the Ganges. From Prayag, the Guru went to Banaras, the centre of Hindu learning and orthodoxy. The Adi Granth describes the many encounters Guru Nanak had with pandits who chided him for his unorthodoxy and probed his knowledge of the sacred texts.

'It matters not how many cartloads of learning you have nor what learned company you keep; it matters not how many boatloads of books you carry nor the tree of knowledge; it matters not how many years or months you spend in study nor with what passion and single-mindedness you pursue knowledge. Only one thing really matters, the rest is but a whirlwind of the ego.'

'And what is the one thing that matters?' they asked.

Nanak replied, 'There are a hundred falsehoods, but this one sovereign truth—that unless truth enters the soul, all service and study is false.'

Nanak was equally forthright about the pandits' fetish of the purity of their cooking vessels and kitchens. He decided to draw their attention to this in his usual manner of highlighting the incongruous aspects.

Nanak went with them and saw with what care they

bathed, scrubbed their utensils, swept the ground near the hearth, washed the vegetables, and cooked the food. When one plate was laid before Nanak, he refused to eat from it. 'I am not satisfied with the purity of the food you offer me. It is prepared by one who is full of sin and sins cannot be cleansed by washing the body.'

The pandits did not fully comprehend the import of Nanak's words and prepared the meal afresh. This time they dug up the earth and replastered it; they even washed the logs of wood before kindling them. Again Nanak refused to partake of the meal and continued his sermon. 'You err in believing that purity can be gained by scrubbing and washing. That does not apply even to inanimate things like wood, dung-fuel or water, much less to a human being. Man is unclean when his heart is tainted with greed, his tongue coated with falsehood, his eyes envious of the beauty of another's wife or his wealth, his ears dirty with slander. All these can only be cleansed by knowledge. Basically all men are good but often they pursue a predetermined path to hell.'

Nanak was questioned on his attitude towards the sacred texts of the Hindus: 'The Vedas say one thing and you another. People who read the Vedas do not follow their teachings and now you confuse them more than ever. Why don't you either combine your teaching with that of the Vedas or separate them more distinctly?'

Nanak replied, 'The Vedas tell you of the difference between good and evil. Sin is the seed of hell, chastity the seed of paradise. Knowledge and the teaching of the Vedas complement each other—they are to one another as merchandise to the merchant.'

It would appear that by this time Nanak had decided that his faith was to be an eclectic one for he sang hymns of Namdev, Kabir, Ravi Das, Sain and Beni.

His new disciples tried to persuade Nanak to settle down in Banaras. Nanak refused to do so. 'I pursue the one and only path of devotion to God,' he replied. 'Your learning and religion do not appeal to me, and I have no interest in trade other than the name of God, for God Himself has extinguished the desire for acquisition in me.'

Piecing together evidence from other sources we find that the first journey apparently took the Guru as far east as Bengal and Assam. On his way back to Punjab, he spent some days at Jagannath Puri. He travelled round Punjab and visited the Sufi headquarters at Pak Pattan before he set out on his second long voyage—this time southwards. He is said to have travelled through Tamil Nadu, Kerala, Konkan and Rajasthan—though there is little evidence to show that he did so.

Nanak sojourned in the Himalayas for some time before he set out on his last and longest journey. This was westwards to the Muslims' holy cities of Mecca and Medina as far as Baghdad. It was on this journey that another incident took place. He was staying in a mosque and fell asleep with his feet towards the Kaaba—an act considered of grave disrespect to the house of God. When the mullah came to say his prayers, he shook Nanak rudely and said: 'O servant of God, thou hast thy feet towards Kaaba, the house of God—why hast thou done such a thing?'

Nanak replied: 'Then turn my feet towards some direction where there is no God nor the Kaaba.'

By the time Nanak returned home, the Mughal Babur had invaded the Punjab. The Guru was at Saidpur when the town was sacked by the invaders. Nanak makes many references to the havoc caused by this invasion.

Nanak was by this time too old to undertake any more strenuous journeys. He settled in the village Kartarpur where he spent the last years of his life preaching to the people. His disciples came to be known as Sikhs. He built a dharamshala (abode of faith) whose inmates followed a strict code of discipline: rising well before dawn, bathing and then foregathering in the dharamshala for prayer and hymn-singing.

They went about their daily chores and met again for the evening service. At the dharamshala was the guru-ka-langar (the guru's kitchen) where all who came were obliged to break bread without distinction of caste or religion.

Among Nanak's disciples was a man called Lehna whom Nanak chose in preference to his sons as his successor. Said Nanak to Lehna: 'Thou art Angad, a part of my body,' and asked another disciple to daub Angad's forehead with saffron and proclaim him the second Guru.

Nanak died in the early hours of the morning of 22 September 1539. He was a poet and lover of nature to the last. As he lay on his deathbed he recalled the scenes of his childhood. 'The tamarisk must be in flower now; the pampas grass must be waving its woolly head in the breeze; the cicadas must be calling in the lonely glades,' he said before he closed his eyes in eternal sleep.

Mehervan's *Janam Sakhi* records the manner his body was laid to rest. Said the Mussalmans: 'We will bury him,' the Hindus: 'We will cremate him.' Nanak said: 'You place flowers on either side, Hindus on my right, Muslims on my left. Those whose flowers remain fresh tomorrow will have their way.' He asked them to pray. When the prayer was over, Nanak pulled the sheet over him and went to eternal sleep. When they raised the sheet the following morning, they found nothing. The flowers of both communities were fresh. The Hindus took theirs; the Muslims took those that they had placed.

# KABIR

Without doubt the most popular saint-poet of northern India was, and is, Bhakta Kabir. Almost everyone, be he Hindu, Muslim, Sikh or Christian, educated or unlettered, rich or poor, will know a doha or two by Kabir by heart. And yet we have no definitive biography of the man. The popular cherished belief is that he was born in Benaras, of Brahmin parents, but was adopted and raised by a Muslim weaver's family. I find that hard to accept. My own reading is that he was the son of a Muslim weaver who was influenced by the teachings of Hindu bhaktas and rose above considerations of caste and religion. In his writings, he always referred to himself as a julaha (weaver).

There are two distinct compilations of Kabir's poems, his granthavali which is an anthology of his dohas known by rote by millions of Indians, and his slokas, incorporated by Guru Arjan in the Adi Granth, that are known to those familiar with the Sikh scriptures. Though the message that comes through is the same, the two read quite differently. While the former have been rendered into English many times, the latter have only been rendered by scholars like Macauliffe, Manmohan Singh, Gopal Singh and Talib as parts of their translations of the Adi Granth. For the first time, the Kabir of the Sikh scriptures has been published in translation in a separate book, *So Spake Kabira*, by Kartar Singh Duggal. He has taken the trouble to render Kabir in poetic form and his translation makes pleasanter reading than the translations of his predecessors. If he had presented the opening lines of the slokas in Roman script, it would have made identification easier.

Duggal is among the top three or four writers in Punjabi; his output of novels, short stories and poems would fill a couple of shelves of a library. Rather late in life he realized that Punjabi could take him only that far but no further. So he switched to English. He is equally prolific in both languages. I can't think of another person who could have done more justice to Kabir than Duggal. He is a devout Sikh; his wife is Muslim.

Kabir (1398–1448) was by no means the founder of the Bhakti movement as stated by Duggal. The movement had started more than a couple of centuries earlier in Tamil Nadu and spread northwards. A popular couplet describes its advent and increase:

## KABIR

Bhakti Dravid oppjee, Uttar Ramanand
Pargat kiyo Kabir nay sapt dyveep nav khand.

(Bhakti was born in Dravidian country; brought north
   by Ramanand;
Kabir spread it over the seven seas and nine continents.)

Kabir's message, in the simplest words, is the total rejection of religious bigotry of any kind. He mocked the pretensions of mullahs and pandits with equal relish, pointed out the futility of erecting mosques and temples for a God who is all-pervasive, and scorned the arrogance of the rich and the powerful who, like the poor and the destitute, must go into oblivion. He asked, 'What is the point of putting bricks and stones together or raise a minaret for the mullah to shout the call for prayer? Has God become hard of hearing? And why bother about the mighty and the rich? They are no better than the date palm which casts a very small shade for the weary traveller and its fruit is far beyond reach.' Kabir accepted the Semitic version of the origin of life and the casteless fraternity of humans:

Aval Allah noor upa ya
Qudrat ke sab bandey
Ek noor te sab jag upjea
Kaun bhaley kaun mandey.

(At first God created light,
We are creatures of nature;

## ON RELIGION

From one light came the entire world
Who then is high and who is low?)

He summed up what the aim of life should be in four memorable lines:

> Jab ham aaye jagat mein,
> Jag hassa ham roey;
> Aisee karnee kar chalen
> Jab ham jaayen jagat say
> Ham hassein jag roey.

(When I was born everyone rejoiced but I did cry
Fill your life with such deeds that
When you die
You have a smile on your lips while others cry.)

# SHRADDHA MATA

Over the years I met Shraddha Mata many times, especially on visits to Jaipur, when I would call on her at the Hathroi Fort. Each meeting was for me a memorable one; I became genuinely fond of her. However, it was the first encounter with her which remains imprinted on my mind.

Like many others, I had read about her in M. O. Mathai's memories of his days with Pandit Nehru. According to Mathai, Panditji had a liaison with Shraddha Mata and fathered an illegitimate child who was born in a Catholic hospital in south India. Shraddha Mata later abandoned the child and returned to Uttar Pradesh to resume her mission as a tantrik sadhvi.

It was Maneka Gandhi's mother, Amteshwar Anand, who told me that if I wanted to meet Shraddha Mata I should go to the Nigambodh Ghat cremation ground.

Several corpses were burning at the ghat, and a few mourners sitting here and there. I asked the timber dealer who supplied wood for cremations for Shraddha Mata's dwelling. He pointed to a platform surrounded by gunny sacks at one end of the ground. I made my way there and saw an elderly lady in a saffron kurta-dhoti sitting cross-legged on a wooden takhtposh counting the beads of her rosary.

'Kaun hai? (Who is it?)' she shouted.

'Aap ke darshan karne aaya hoon (I have come for your darshan),' I replied.

'Darshan to karne aaya hai, tera naam bhi to hai koi? (You have come for darshan, but don't you have a name?)'

I mentioned my name. 'Are you the same fellow who was editor of *The Illustrated Weekly of India*?'

I admitted I was. She exploded: 'Jhootha kahin ka! (You are a liar!) Darshan parshan nahin. You want to know more about what that haramzada Mathai has written about me. It is all a pack of lies.'

'But you met Panditji many times,' I ventured.

'Yes, many times. He wrote many letters to me. If he had married again, he would certainly have married me. I put him in his place. I told him "Yeh my dear nahin chalega (addressing me as my dear in your letters won't do). You are a Brahmin, I am a Kshatriya. How can there be anything more than friendship between us?"'

'How is it that Indiraji does not know anything about you?'

'Bewakoof? Koi aisi baat apne beti ko batata hai? (Fool, will any father tell his daughter such things?)'

I was cut down to size. When she beckoned to me to sit down on the floor, my feet touched her wooden sandals.

'Sadhvi ke khadaon ko pair lagaata hai! Tameez nahin hai? (You touch the sandals of a sadhvi! Don't you have any manners?)'

I apologized and sat down. She asked me, 'Tu ishwar mein vishwas nahin karta? (Don't you believe in God?)'

I admitted I did not. 'Bahut ghamand hai tere mein. (You are full of pride.) Isi liye itna bakwass likhta hai. (That is why you write such rubbish.)'

She invited me to spend some time with her at the Hathroi Fort in Jaipur, so as to teach me how to write. She spoke for over an hour. Her tone changed to one of affection. I was enchanted by her rough, loving tone. When I took her leave, I touched her feet and received her blessings. It was too dark for me to see what she looked like.

A few weeks later I went to Jaipur—the photographer Raghu Rai was with me. Armed with a basket of fruit, we arrived at the Hathroi Fort: it was in fact a miniature fortress atop a hill overlooking the All India Radio Station and the city of Jaipur. As haunted a place as I have ever seen. There were lots of dogs and snakes about. We climbed the stairs to the first floor. Shraddha Mata was sitting on a charpoy, with four puppies playing at her feet. We touched her feet. As ordered by her, we took the basket of fruit to the tower where there was a temple. Shraddha Mata was known to spend her nights there practising tantra.

While Raghu Rai got busy clicking photographs, I sat at her feet and had a good look at her. She must have then been in her seventies—light-skinned and full-bosomed. In her younger days she must have been stunningly beautiful. From the time she became a sadhvi she took to wearing a leopard skin round her middle, weaving her hair in a chignon like those seen in pictures of Lord Shiva and carrying a trishul in her hand. To the anglicized Nehru, she must have looked like an incarnation of the Mother India of his fantasies.

It was at the Lucknow circuit house that Panditji invited her over one evening after his day's work was done. Panditji did what any man would have done to an attractive young woman dressed in no more than a leopard skin. When she wrote to him of its consequences, Panditji stopped writing to her. Nobody knows whether she bore him a son or a daughter, or what became of him or her.

Shraddha Mata was more taken up by Raghu Rai than me. He was, as he is still, a handsome fellow. She invited him to spend the night at the Hathroi Fort to get the atmosphere of the place. Raghu funked accepting her invitation.

## SHRADDHA MATA

The next time I called on Shraddha Mata was in winter. She was having a bath in a tub placed on the parapet. She shouted to me to sit down in the verandah outside her bedroom. I could see her from where I sat. She continued talking loudly as she rubbed herself dry with a towel. It was very titillating.

She came away looking fresh and cheerful. She had been abroad meeting her disciples.

She invited me to spend the night in the fortress. Like Raghu Rai, I too funked accepting her offer.

I wrote several pieces on her. Among the many letters I received, one was from a lawyer in Bareilly who claimed to be her husband. He offered to tell me everything about Shraddha Mata if I gave him a large sum of money. He ended his letter saying, 'This woman was not even born a virgin.'

I asked Shraddha Mata about this man. She dismissed him with scorn. She told me she was born into a zamindar family (very distantly related to Union Minister for External Affairs Dinesh Singh). As a child she was named Parvati but was addressed as Bacchasahib.

After she became a sadhvi, she took on the name Shraddha Devi Jijnasu. Everyone called her Shraddha Mata. She had been given away in marriage at the age of twelve. She refused to live with her husband and instead went off to join Gandhiji who advised her to return to her husband or her parents. She did neither; she turned into a sadhvi.

Although I met Shraddha Mata no more than six or seven times, each meeting was for me a memorable occasion. I have never met a more unusual woman.

# MOTHER VALIKAMMA

As I bent low to touch her feet, she hauled me by my shoulders and took me in her embrace. She kissed me on both sides of my chest, murmuring, 'Namo Shivaye, Namo Shivaye!' It was a warm, sensuous hug; I had to hold back my tears. She addressed me as her son, my wife as her daughter. Both of us were a lot older than her parents. This was the thirty-six-year-old Sadhvi, worshipped by millions of her devotees as Mata Amritanandmayi. To her fellow villagers of Vallicava, she is Valimma. Vallicava lies along the Arabian seacoast on the Cochin–Trivandrum highway. The route is marked with red flags, pictures of Karl Marx, Lenin and Stalin. This is a communist country with its base at Alleppey. About 20 miles south of the helipad, you branch off to the right. This is Lord Krishna's country presided over by Ma Amritanandmayi. The road ends at a broad canal. You hire a boat to take you across to the math.

While I waited for the appointed time for darshan, Narayanan of the *Malayala Manorama* briefed me on Mata's background. She is the second daughter of a family of eight children belonging to a tribe of fisher-folk. She was born on 27 November 1953. She was a precocious child and was able to talk when only six months old. And run around before she was two. She went to school, studied up to Class V and then she found she knew more than was required for Class X. She gave up. She was wayward and often went into trances. Her parents got tired of her. She moved over to her uncle's but soon decided to live on her own, making her ends meet by stitching clothes.

She was uncommonly attractive and many suitors sought her hand. Then she was fully absorbed in the world of meditation. She also saw herself as Kanya Kumari and decided to remain unmarried. Some of the many young men who were drawn to her, took a vow of Brahmacharya and stayed on with her. Needless to say, much gossip and scandal was spread about the goings on in this math. She ignored it. Many scandals attributed to her: how she turned water into milk; gave tulsi leaves to fishermen to get more than their usual catch; how while in a trance she was declared dead for eight hours. She no longer indulges in performing miracles. Her chief miracle, as I said before, is the enormous warmth which emanates from her body.

My first question to her was, 'How can one overcome the fear of death?' Her answer was translated for me: 'Body is physical and must perish on death. But life continues. It is like an electric bulb which fuses but the current continues. If you cut your finger, it will not heal by simply looking at it. You have to apply medicine to it. If you fear death, find the means of overcoming that fear. Anyhow, why do you ask me questions to which you know the answers?'

'I ask because I do not know, I do not believe in life hereafter because there is no evidence to support it,' I replied.

'You cannot totally rule it out,' she continued. 'In any case, it serves a useful social purpose. You tell a child that if he lies, he will go blind. It is not true but a useful ploy to keep it on the path of truth.'

'There may be some justification to keep the illiterate masses on the right path by frightening them of consequences. But that does not apply to a thinking person. I am quite happy to admit I do not know.'

She smiled—she smiles most of the time—and replied, 'It is not only through personal experiences that you realize everything. You have to accept the experiences of sages and rishis who train themselves to attain mystic knowledge. Take a simple example. Mix sugar with white sand. You will not be able to sift one from the other but an ant will unerringly take the sugar and leave out the sand.'

I changed the topic. 'I don't need God to make me good. We can derive sustenance from others without believing in God.'

'Denying God is like lying on the ground and spitting to the sky. The spit will only fall on your face.' She replied gently but firmly.

'If there is God, tell me why bad things happen to good people?' She replied, 'To the God-fearing, it is fate, it is punishment for evil deeds done in past lives. To the non-believer, it is an accident. If a child is born blind, the believer will ascribe it to sins committed in its previous life, the non-believer in some hormonal deficiency in the parents.'

One of my security guards interrupted the dialogue. 'Mata, do you believe in heaven and hell?'

'Heaven and hell are here on this earth. You do something bad and your presence will make life a living hell,' she replied.

We had taken more than the time allotted to us. I moved myself from the marble floor and touched her feet. Once more she took me in her embrace and kissed me tenderly, murmuring, 'Namo Shivaye, Namo Shivaye!' And once more, I had to hold back my tears. As I turned around, I saw a sallow European girl, who had been standing like a marble statue at the door, take ice-cubes out of a flask and gently rub Mata's face, lips and arms with them. I was told that every encounter Mata has with people raises her body temperature to dangerous levels. She takes on their ailments and sins upon herself. Having been a sinner all my life, she must have required a lot of ice-cubes to get rid of the fever that contact with me must have brought on her.

## AFTER LIFE

As the time for my own departure draws near, I find myself more and more tempted to believe in an afterlife: will I be around in the world twenty years from now in new vestments as the Gita assures me? And what will I be reborn as—a cat, dog, serpent, rat or worm as punishment for what I have done in this life? Or return as a glamorous film star or the future prime minister of Hindustan for the few good things I have done? Or am I to be extinguished like a lamp, never to be relit? I am more than willing to lend my ears to hear answers to these questions. It was in this state of uncertainty that I went to hear Swami Atmanand's discourse on Punarjanma (rebirth).

The large auditorium was packed. For one hour and a half, over a thousand men and women heard Swamiji in rapt attention. I have never heard Hindi better spoken and arguments put with greater clarity, marshalling knowledge of the past and the present. I will put his arguments as I took them down in my notebook along with my own comments.

The concept of birth-death and rebirth is unique to Indian-born religions: Hinduism, Jainism, Buddhism and Sikhism, said Swamiji. He is only partially correct because some Greek philosophers have also expressed similar views. But he is substantially correct inasmuch as the Hebraic family of religions: Judaism, Christianity and Islam, though they have the concept of the Day of Judgement, when the dead will rise from their graves, subscribe only to one life, not an unending cycle of birth, death and rebirth as we do.

Swamiji then proceeded to explain that there are three ways of acquiring knowledge. First, through one of our five senses (pratyaksh pramaan); second by inference (anumaan pramaan); and finally from inspired texts or people with divine knowledge (agam pramaan). In the third category are our Vedas, Upanishads, Gita, as well as rishis and sages like Vivekananda and Sri Ramakrishna Paramhansa. He said that knowledge of rebirth could not be acquired by the senses. I am in agreement with him. He went on to say that all our sacred texts as well as our prophets and seers accepted the theory of instant rebirth after death. Once again I agree with him that they said so.

But this is not good enough for unbelievers like me because I refuse to accept anyone's word for something I should discover for myself.

We are left with only one of the three means of acquiring this knowledge viz. by inference (anumaan pramaan). For conclusive proof, Swami Atmanand cited the research carried out by Dr H. N. Bannerjee, director of the erstwhile Institute of Parapsychology of the University of Rajashtan. Bannerjee's book on the subject listed cases of children who recalled incidents of their previous births which, according to Swamiji, were all found to be authentic. I also read Bannerjee's book and met him. I have not the slightest hesitation in saying that not one of the cases cited by him could be established as authentic. Rajasthan University itself ordered the institute to be wound up and instituted proceedings against Bannerjee. The so-called research into parapsychology, extrasensory perception (ESP) was found to be a massive hoax. Swamiji maintained that the breakthrough in knowledge, like Newton's discovery of the law of gravity, did not come through trial and error but by what Einstein described as 'intuitive flight'. He may be right. But that does not forward the argument for rebirth because children between the ages of two and seven, who apparently have peeps into their past lives, do not have 'intuitional flights' productive of anything except fantasies.

To clinch the argument, Swamiji posed the question:

## AFTER LIFE

why are some born in rich homes, others in poor houses? Why are some born healthy, others blind or sickly? If we accept the theory of only one life, we cannot explain such god-inflicted injustice. Ergo, there must be a cycle of births whereby God punishes or rewards people for what they have done in one life by squaring their karmas in the next. I am sorry Swamiji, this does not convince me at all. I am happy to wallow in my ignorance and admit, I do not know where I come from, why I am here, and where I will go when I die.

> Myself when young did eagerly frequent
> Doctor and saint and heard great argument
> About it and about: but ever more
> Came out by the same door as I went.

# ACKNOWLEDGEMENTS

The literary estate of Khushwant Singh and the publishers thank Penguin Books India for permission to reprint the following copyright material:

'Religion: A Personal View' (appearing originally as 'On Religion'); and 'Kabir', from *Why I Supported the Emergency: Essays and Profiles*.